WATER *at the* ROOTS

WATER
at the
ROOTS

Poems and Insights
of a Visionary Farmer

PHILIP BRITTS

Edited by Jennifer Harries

PLOUGH PUBLISHING HOUSE

Published by Plough Publishing House
Walden, New York
Robertsbridge, England
Elsmore, Australia
www.plough.com

Plough produces books, a quarterly magazine, and Plough.com to encourage people and help them put their faith into action. We believe Jesus can transform the world and that his teachings and example apply to all aspects of life. At the same time, we seek common ground with all people regardless of their creed.

Plough is the publishing house of the Bruderhof, an international community of families and singles seeking to follow Jesus together. Members of the Bruderhof are committed to a way of radical discipleship in the spirit of the Sermon on the Mount. Inspired by the first church in Jerusalem (Acts 2 and 4), they renounce private property and share everything in common in a life of nonviolence, justice, and service to neighbors near and far. To learn more about the Bruderhof's faith, history, and daily life, see Bruderhof.com. (Views expressed by Plough authors are their own and do not necessarily reflect the position of the Bruderhof.)

ISBN: 978-0-87486-128-0
22 21 20 19 18   1 2 3 4 5 6 7 8

Cover image, *Golden Beets*, by Yara Anderson. Reproduced by permission of the artist. Photographs of Hiroshima and Bristol are in the public domain. Artwork on pages iii, vii, and 162 by Asuka Hishiki. Used by permission. All other photographs copyright Plough Publishing House.

A catalog record for this book is available from the British Library.
Library of Congress Cataloging-in-Publication Data
Names: Britts, Philip, 1917-1949, author. | Harries, Jennifer, editor. |
   Kline, David, writer of foreword.
Title: Water at the roots : poems and insights of a visionary farmer / Philip
   Britts ; edited by Jennifer Harries ; foreword by David Kline.
Description: Walden, New York : Plough Publishing House, [2017] | Includes
   index.
Identifiers: LCCN 2017030974 (print) | LCCN 2017041087 (ebook) | ISBN
   9780874861297 (epub) | ISBN 9780874861303 (mobi) | ISBN 9780874861327 (
   pdf) | ISBN 9780874861280 (pbk.)
Classification: LCC PR6003.R3866 (ebook) | LCC PR6003.R3866 A6 2017 (print) |
   DDC 821/.912--dc23
LC record available at https://lccn.loc.gov/2017030974

Printed in the United States of America

Faith is like water at the roots.

PHILIP BRITTS

CONTENTS

Philip Britts,
Caacupé,
1943

FOREWORD

DAVID KLINE

I wish I could have met Philip Britts. Not only was he
a prolific writer and poet, a pastor, an astute observer
of his natural surroundings, and, to use a phrase of his,
a steward of the mysteries of God; he was also a true
landsman. Although I was only a child when Philip died,
it is here, as a farmer, that I immediately connect with
this gifted man. While I am not a trained horticulturist as
Philip was, I too am a keeper of the orchard. I plant and
prune and harvest.

As editor of *Farming Magazine,* I often receive letters
from readers in cities. One in the Bronx wrote, "I don't
have a farm, but my heart is there. I grow tomato plants
in a window box." Philip's words are also for people like
this; he knew that even though most people do not have
land to farm and cannot grow the food they eat, everyone
hungers, at least at some level, for a connection with
nature. And he saw this hunger in the context of a related
problem: our disconnectedness from one another. As he
wrote in one essay:

> Man's relationship to the land must be true and just,
> but it is only possible when his relationship to his fellow

man is true and just and organic. This includes the relationship of all the activities of man, the relationship of industry with agriculture, of science with art, the relationship between sexes, and above all, the relationship between man's spiritual life and his material life.

One of the great tragedies of the modern world is the complete divorce of the city dwellers from nature and the land. . . .

The decisive factor in the success of the farmer will be, ultimately, the love of farming. This love comes when we find, not in nature, but through and behind nature, that something which impels worship and service. Part of the glory of farming is that indescribable sensation that comes, perhaps rarely, when one walks through a field of alfalfa in the morning sun, when one smells earth after rain, or when one watches the ripples on a field of wheat; the sensation hinted at by the poet, when his

> *Restless ploughman pauses, turns and wondering,*
> *Deep beneath his rustic habit, finds himself a king.*[*]

This love is fed by understanding, by knowledge. Without going the whole way with Leonardo da Vinci and his "perfect knowledge is perfect love," the more one knows of the mysteries of the earth the better one can love farming in the sense of giving one's service to it.

It is obvious that Philip Britts lived the life he wrote about. He knew that working with nature and her seasons matters, that farming is not just a matter of tilling the land but loving it, of nurturing instead of exploiting it. Despite his short life, he lived fully and generously. What he wrote seven decades ago is as pertinent today as when he wrote it, perhaps even more so in this greed-driven

[*]   A.E. (George William Russell), "Earth Breath."

society where many thoughtful people are looking at intentional community and sustainable living as alternatives to consumerism.

Philip, I think, would argue that while we can promote such alternatives regardless of where we live, it is best to move not just spiritually but also physically from places of decadence. Maybe not to a cave in the mountains, but to the land, where one can be nurtured and be a nurturer in return. Where one can, like Elijah, in quietness, in the natural world, listen to the voice of God.

I wonder what Philip would have to say about today's agribusiness, or about the mindset that believes technology will solve all the world's food production problems. Philip clearly believed in exercising caution: before welcoming a new agricultural development simply because it is scientifically plausible or commercially profitable, we ought to take care to avoid or diminish any moral harm it might cause. One cannot help thinking here of genetically engineered plants developed to allow minimum tillage, which have led to millions of acres of farmland being soaked with herbicides.

Philip's writings indicate that he understood what Omar Bradley meant when he said, "Technology is a useful servant but a dangerous master." Although many of us do not live in an intentional community like Philip and his family did, we can heed his wisdom and take steps to control technology to the point that it doesn't displace our neighbor.

Philip's writings remind me of the farming community I grew up in. My father was a thresher for many years. At one point he worked for twenty-five neighbors, spending day after day at their farms threshing, husking corn,

hulling clover, and filling silos with corn. Those neigh-
bors – Methodists, Catholics, Mennonites, Lutherans,
and Amish – all shared their labor for the common good.
As I told my father, he probably saw the best years of
American agriculture, a period when there was enough
technology to lighten your load but not enough to replace
your neighbor. When my father lay dying, I would turn
to his diaries from his years as an active farmer, and read
from them to him. "Yes, yes," he would remember; and
he would smile.

But back to the poetry that forms the heart of this book:
in spite of the many hardships Philip and his community
weathered in leaving his native England and hacking
out a livelihood in the harsh wilderness of Paraguay,
poetry never stopped flowing out of him, like water from
a spring. With Wendell Berry, he believed that "life is a
miracle." And as his last poem, "Toucan," shows, he never
lost his youthful sense of wonder:

> The boy there,
> Standing, staring,
> Staring at the bird –
> Eyes alight, breath held,
> Bare toes gripping the sand,
> Wonder-held.
> The boy there,
> Standing, staring –
> That's my son –
> A sound from me
> And he will turn,
> Dart to me,
> "Daddy, did you see?"

Reading Philip's prose and poetry, you feel the kinship he had with all living things around him, both human and wild. His ability to see into the mysteries of their lives reminds me of what I have read of the Lakota Sioux. They knew that, removed from nature, a person's heart becomes hard; and that lack of respect for living things soon leads to lack of respect for one's fellow humans too. Philip kept himself close to the softening influence of nature.

To be sure, Philip's poetry also reveals his total commitment to Christ as Lord of his life. He believed the Sermon on the Mount where it reads, "Seek ye first the kingdom of God, and his righteousness; and all these things shall be added unto you" (Matt. 6:33), and he trusted the promise of the Psalmist, who wrote, "I will both me lay down in peace, and sleep: for thou, Lord, only makest me dwell in safety" (Ps. 4:8). And yet this belief in God and in the goodness of creation did not make Philip self-satisfied. On the contrary, whether writing poetry, farming, or probing the science behind it, he kept grappling with the question, "How shall we live?" It is this tireless search that gives him undiminished relevance so many years after his early death and makes his contributions as a poet and a lover of the land deserving of as wide an audience as possible.

David Kline, an Amish organic farmer in Ohio, has written three books: *Letters from Larksong, Great Possessions,* and *Scratching the Woodchuck.*

TO THE READER

JENNIFER HARRIES

> Let this be the way that I go,
> And the life that I try,
> My feet being firm in the field,
> And my heart in the sky.

Who was Philip Britts? His life was short, and his
biographical details are easily summed up: He was a
farmer and pastor, a husband and father. Born in 1917
in Devon, England, he became a pacifist and joined the
Bruderhof, a Christian community. During the Second
World War he moved to South America, where, in 1949,
he died of a tropical illness at the age of thirty-one,
leaving a widow with three young children and a fourth
on the way.

The Bruderhof started in 1920 in Germany. Inspired
by the first Christians, members hold property in
common and try to follow Christ wholeheartedly,
living out Jesus' words in the Sermon on the Mount. In
1937, Hitler's government expelled the community and
its members fled to England, where an offshoot of the
original group had started a community on a farm in the

Costwolds the previous year. It was here that Philip and
his wife Joan joined, as did my parents and I. From that
time on, Philip's story and that of the community were
intertwined.

Philip was a tall, thoughtful man, not given to many
words; throughout his life, he retained the typical West
Country speech of the Devon farmer, slow and deliberate.
He loved the work on the land and the mystery of
growing things. For him to be part of creation was joy – to
work with nature, not against it, and "to see in growing
corn the fingerprints of God."

After Philip died, his friends began, from time to time,
to receive gifts from his young widow: poems that she
had found and collected after his death, and copied out
for them.

Most of Philip's poems and essays have never been
published before. Why now? His generation faced
great dangers and upheavals, but so does ours. Philip's
response to his own age's trials – to root himself in God
and dedicate himself to a community and to the land he
farmed – speaks to our age. Perhaps this is particularly
true because his community was itself driven from
country to country and continent to continent, and
because the earth he tilled was not the West Country
soil of his birthplace. His story is not a romantic agrarian
elegy, a throwback, but a real human life lived in the
thick of history.

Today, Philip Britts's record of his experience of the
natural world is particularly poignant because we are,
perhaps even more than he was, aware of the fragility
of that world and of our role in stewarding it. Pope
Francis has called our use of nature "indiscriminate and

tyrannical." In his encyclical *Laudato si'* he writes, "The violence present in our hearts, wounded by sin, is also reflected in the symptoms of sickness evident in the soil, in the water, in the air and in all forms of life." Elsewhere, he has pointed out that "an economic system centred on the god of money needs to plunder nature to sustain the frenetic rhythm of consumption that is inherent to it. The monopolising of lands, deforestation, the appropriation of water . . . are some of the evils that tear man from the land of his birth."

Today, time-tested social structures and moral teachings are being cast off, even trampled on. New wars erupt before old ones have ceased. And technological changes threaten to uproot us from the natural world. In a world of concrete and smartphones, we find ourselves craving reality.

Philip Britts shows us where and how we can slake that thirst. Later writers have shared his sense, best expressed in his poems, that nature is not just nature, but points to something mysterious and profound beyond itself. Rachel Carson, Annie Dillard, Abraham Joshua Heschel, Paul Brand, and many others have sought to express the sense of awe, the link to the transcendent, that they find in the natural world. Wendell Berry writes about life as "miracle and mystery," and Albert Einstein says, "One cannot help but be in awe when one contemplates the mysteries of eternity, of life, of the marvellous structure of reality. It is enough if one tries merely to comprehend a little of this mystery every day."

But this is a mystery always at hand, an everyday miracle. As a farmer, Philip experienced this awe in the same soil that meant rootedness and hard work. And his concern was never merely reconnecting to the land, as though that alone could heal us. Rather, he saw that in losing connection to the land, we are losing our humanity and our connection to each other, and that by losing our connection to the created world we are losing an avenue of awareness of the Creator. As a pastor, he read the book of nature together with the book of scripture, allowing them to illuminate each other: "Faith is like water at the roots," he writes. "If we have faith, we can face the sun, we can turn the heat and the light into life-giving fruits, into love. . . . Faith is a gift like the rain, and like the rain it is something to be watched for and prayed for and waited for."

Philip's times saw many proposed solutions to the problems he witnessed, but after looking at the major movements of the day – the peace movement and socialism, among others – he found his answer closer to home: not in farming for its own sake, but in an attempt to live out his faith and the radical teachings of Jesus on a very personal and local level in an intentional community on the land. This was boots-on-the-ground discipleship, as he travelled with the community to a country far from that of his birth. And as you will see, it would cost him his life.

You will get to know Philip best by reading his own words. The backbone of this book, therefore, is a selection of his poems arranged roughly chronologically, with other writings of his interspersed. I have given these poems and writings context by telling the story of the man who wrote them. Philip was a family friend and a fellow member of the Bruderhof movement, and I have supplemented archival records with my own memories.

(My thanks to Miriam Mathis and Carole Vanderhoof, whose research made this book possible.) In keeping with Philip's poems, I have used British spelling throughout the book. Philip's words appear in black.

Philip Britts died young and in relative obscurity, but his vision continues to guide the community he helped lead through some of the most challenging years of its history. May Philip's poetry and insights also inspire you, the reader, in your own quest for deeper roots and greater wonder, and a practical way of life that makes both possible.

Jennifer Harries, a member of the Bruderhof, was born in Llansamlet, Wales. Having taught elementary school for decades, she now mentors younger teachers. She lives in New York.

Bristol, England,
city center, 1920s

WILDERNESS

CHAPTER I

Look up to see if the God I serve has seen

The town of Honiton, in Devon, southwest England, is surrounded by rich farmland. The River Otter flows nearby, leading down to the sea some ten miles to the south. Footpaths trace their way through the countryside. Here Philip Herbert Cootes Britts was born on April 17, 1917, and it was here that his lifelong love of farming and nature, hiking and camping, poetry and song first took root.

By the time he was four, though, his family had moved to a suburb of Bristol, a busy port city famed equally for its cathedral and its urban poverty. Here, his sister Molly was born.

Most of Philip's childhood memories were centred on Bristol, which was plagued by crime and unrest at the time, but from early on he preferred the countryside.

Philip went to grammar school and then looked for any kind of work to earn money for his university studies. He worked in a quarry, then took care of a wealthy man's orchid house. Later in life, Philip would tell stories about his escapades during these years. One ended in a major motorcycle accident that proved to be a turning point in his life.

Little more is known of his early life, but his earliest
poems give a window into his thoughts.

ALONE

When the night is cold and the winds complain,
And the pine trees sigh for the coming rain,
I will light a lonely watch-fire, near by a lonely wood,
And look up to see if the God I serve has seen and
understood.
I'll watch the wood-ash whitened by the licking yellow
tongues,
I'll watch the wood-smoke rising, sweet smoke that
stings the lungs,
See the leaping, laughing watch-fire throw shadows on
the grass,
See the rushes bend and tremble to let the shadows pass,
While my soul flies through the forest, back a trail of
weary years,
And the clouds, as if in pity, shed their tears.
Oh, I do not want their pity for a trail that's closed
behind,
Though all the things on earth combine to play upon
the mind.
I must keep on riding forward to a goal I'll never find –
What matter the eyes have seen so much that the soul is
colour-blind?

1934

It's not difficult to see the influence of the popular poets of the day – William Butler Yeats, John Masefield, A. E. Housman – on the young Philip's work.

"I SENT MY SOUL SEARCHING"

I sent my soul searching the songs of the ages,
The hearts of all poets were bared to my eyes,
Though I read golden thoughts as I turned golden pages
The echoes fell faint as of songs that were sighs.

I weighed up the greatness of all who were greatest
Whom the world had called strong and the world had
    called wise,
But the song that they sang from the first to the latest
Fell back from the portals of thy Paradise.

1934

Am I dreaming this wilderness?

Philip's spiritual search did not cut him off from the political and social drama of his time and place. Rather, his questions thrust him into the heart of things. The 1930s were turbulent years for Europe and beyond, years of uncertainty and disillusionment. Socialism and a strong peace movement in England held promise, but rumours from Russia soon cast shadows on communism, and economic meltdown on the West's own grand visions of humankind's continuous progress.

This suffering soon struck close to Philip. Not far from Bristol, on the other side of the River Severn estuary, are the coal-mining valleys of South Wales. These valleys were hard hit during the Great Depression. There were hunger marches from 1922 to 1936, some nationwide, some local, to appeal to the government for help. In 1931 a hunger march of 112 people–many from the Rhondda Valley–marched to Bristol, their slogan "Struggle or starve." The demonstration was broken up by mounted police.

WORKING IN A CITY

There are so many songs that need to be sung.
There are so many beautiful things that await
The sensitive hand to pick them up
From this strange din of busy living.

I hear an echo in my sleep,
But I, caught up in the tide, like the rest,
Must spend all my life for the means to live:
I starve if I stop to sing –
Yet this dull murmuring
Will keep my heart forever hungering.

1936

The news from abroad was troubling as well. In 1936 both
Hitler and Mussolini were consolidating their power.
Germany and Italy, the Axis Powers, became allies. In
March 1936, Hitler moved twenty thousand troops into
the German Rhineland. Europe was on edge.

WHILE WE RE-ARM

Behind the mountains of imagination,
Screened off by passing mirth and passing tears,
The mind of mortal man is holding unawares
The harvest of a million weary years.

Some time, some place, some unsuspected dreamer
Will catch an echo of the far refrain,
And by his visions in a night of watching,
Will break the misty barriers of the brain.

His song shall shake the souls of politicians,
And while the craven church still watches, dumb,
The hands of men shall grasp at tools, not weapons,
And womanhood shall sing that peace has come.

1936

SANCTUARY

I may not move, while that lone tuft of cloud
Still holds the fairy hues,
An opal thrown against the sky;
And were this shovel in my hand a waiting sword,
And all the great crusaders beckoned me –
I could not move, until the glory passed.

1936

UPON A HILL IN THE MORNING

The timid kiss of the winter sun,
The waiting faith of the naked trees,
The breath of a day so well begun,
Take what you will and leave me these.

Leave me my love and leave me these,
Leave me a soul to feel them still,
Better to be a tramp, who sees,
Than a monarch blind upon a hill.

1936

THE DREAMER

I stood in flowers, knee high,
Dreaming of gentleness,
Dreams, in the promise of a shining sky
That I should make a garden from a wilderness;
I would subdue the soil and make it chaste,
Making the desert bear, the useless good,
With my own strength I would redeem the waste,
Would grow the lily where the thistle stood.

The while I dreamed, the flowers were sweet,
Now that the flowers are gone, it seems
They never bloomed except in dreams.
There are no blossoms at my feet,
The bald blue sky is lustreless,
The flowers had never been, except in dreams,
It was a dream . . . this is a wilderness.

My eyes are tired of the skyline,
My feet are tired of the sand,
I am as dried of laughter as the sun-scorched land,
As the staff in my sun-scorched hand.

Had I not dreamed so long,
Not dreamed of so much beauty, or such grace,
Mayhap I could have trod a quieter path,
With other men, in a green, quieter place . . .

My ears are tired of the silence,
My heart is tired of the toil.
If I sowed any seeds, they have perished,
Nothing is living in the soil.

From the dewless morn I have been here,
Now the day is nearly through;
The tyrant sun sinks down at last,
The colours fade, the sun departs.
Was there a glory – or was that a dream?

I hear, or think I hear, faint music:
Not the song of birds, which are fled from me,
Not the humming of bees, on dream blossom,
Not the voices of happy men . . .
I strain to catch the sound again . . .
Oh! let the music swell, slowly,
Mould a stately music, to soothe the pulse of the earth,
Develop the theme –
Do I pray? or hope? or dream?

I do not know if I dreamed I stood in a garden.
(Was it a dream, the flowers' caress?)
Or did I dream of the sun and the sand –
Am I dreaming this wilderness?

1937

But while both spiritual and political questions demanded
answers, there were others of a more personal nature to
be asked as well. Philip had known Joan Grayling, his
future wife, since childhood. We can surmise she is the
muse in Philip's sometimes stormy poems of love.

DISTRUST

He saw the clouds creep up in stormy herds,
He saw clouds hiding the eternal tors
And clouds like a flock of wild white birds
Winging across the sky towards the moors.
Walking alone he saw the high clouds reeling
In the changing skies,
But his eyes were afraid and seeking,
The voice in his heart was speaking,
And he felt that the clouds were a ceiling
Darkly forbidding his petulant spirit to rise.
Solitude mocked silently.
Sickened, he asked, "Oh, has she faith in me –
The faith that makes men heroes?"
Long after the echo, came a faint reply:
"Find in yourself a faith as true,
Faith is made, not of talk, but deeds,
Lest she go loving on, but you –
Go back to a harvest of weeds."

1936

If we should walk in moonlight,
My valentine and I,
In slow step, by a stream of stars
Where water lilies lie:
Where the elm trees stand in silence
Down the hill like a line of kings,
And alone, in a world that listens,
The nightingale sings:
Sweet the smell of the meadow,
Cool the kiss of the breeze,
A dainty foot and a steady foot,
Step slowly under the trees.
If we should walk in moonlight,
While we and our love are young,
We should hear a softer music
Than the nightingale has sung.

1937

We heard a call and hurried here

Philip graduated from the University of Bristol in the spring of 1939. Now he had a degree in horticulture and a title: Fellow of the Royal Horticultural Society. He seemed poised to enter a secure position in one of England's institutions of learning and research. In June he and Joan were married. The couple moved into a beautiful stone house with a walled garden, which they had recently purchased.

But war was in the air, and Philip had meanwhile become a convinced pacifist. What was he to do if he was called up for military service?

Philip was not alone in his stance. The Peace Pledge Union, founded in 1936, asked its members to sign this statement: "War is a crime against humanity. I renounce war, and am therefore determined not to support any kind of war. I am also determined to work for the removal of all causes of war." The Great War had been "the war to end all wars," but all the blood and sacrifice seemed only to usher in new bloodshed. In her autobiographical *Testament of Youth*, Vera Brittain recounted the losses of her generation, to conclude: "Never again." Philip had joined the Peace Pledge Union (PPU) in 1938, participating with great enthusiasm. He spoke about war and peace in Sunday school classes and started a local PPU chapter in 1939. Joan shared his faith and his commitment to peace.

News from the Continent got worse. Hitler's annexation of Austria in 1938 was followed by his invasion of Poland on September 1, 1939. Two days later Britain declared war on Germany.

Winston Churchill gave rousing speeches: "We are fighting to save the whole world from the pestilence of Nazi tyranny and in defense of all that is most sacred to man. . . . It is a war, viewed in its inherent quality, to establish, on impregnable rocks, the rights of the individual, and it is a war to establish and revive the stature of man."

The peace movement caved in. Hundreds broke their pledge never to support war again and threw their energy into defending England. Even the chapter of the Peace Pledge Union that Philip had started succumbed to the militant mood sweeping the country: most members rushed to defend the homeland against Hitler's threatened invasion.

Then came a real blow: England's churches followed suit, joining its politicians in calling on the populace to support the war effort. But as lonely as Philip and Joan felt in their commitment to peace, they would not yield. They still hoped that it was not too late to avert war.

INSANITY

We see mad scientists watching tubes and flasks,
Staring at fluids with the power of death;
Mad engineers that work out guns of steel
And make great bombs that carry poison breath.

We hear mad statesmen speak of peace through arms,
We read wild praises of the power that rends;
And in the pulpits of the church of Christ
Mad clergy tell us to destroy our friends.

We hear the drone of planes that townsmen build
To scatter death and terror in the town;
And hear the roar of tanks on country roads
That will mow down our brothers, crush them down.

Lest this should happen, still more ships are launched;
To ward off war, we spend more gold on arms,
And lest the voice of Christ is heard to groan,
We sound, more loudly, still more wild alarms.

UNDATED

England was mobilising. In May 1939 Parliament had
passed the Military Training Act: twenty-one- and
twenty-two-year old men could expect to be called up for
six months of military service. The day war was declared,
all men between the ages of eighteen and forty-one
became liable for call-up.

Philip had dreamt of "so much beauty" and of "making
a garden in the wilderness," but what did the God he
served want him to do in the realities of everyday life – in
"the din of busy living" and the preparations for war?

Several years later, Philip told a story of this time: He had been in church listening to the minister. Suddenly the sermon became a call to arms, fanning patriotism, praising heroism, referring to Germans as monsters. Philip rose from his pew, walked quietly up to the pulpit, and asked the minister, in the slow, deliberate way that farmers have, whether he could give him a few minutes to address the congregation. The minister agreed, and Philip spoke: "Jesus said we should love our enemies."

And then, one day in the fall of 1939, Philip and Joan read a newspaper article about a pacifist group in England whose members tried to live by the Sermon on the Mount, following the example of the early church. At this community, the Bruderhof, which had been recently expelled by the Nazis, Britons and Germans were living and working together as brothers and sisters. Was this what they had been looking for? Philip and Joan had to find out for themselves. That October, they cycled twenty-seven miles to the Cotswold Bruderhof. They stayed for a week and decided to return. Here was a way forward, an answer to their search.

> "The kingdom of heaven is like treasure hidden in a
> field, which someone found and hid; then in his joy he
> goes and sells all that he has and buys that field" (Matt.
> 13:44). Sells all that he has – nothing less is sufficient, all is
> nothing compared with the treasure. Let the field be the
> divine counsel of God. Hidden within it the treasure –
> the kingdom – the precious secret of the field.

In November 1939 Philip and Joan sold their house, left family and friends, and moved to the Cotswold community. Giving away all his possessions and launching into an uncertain future, Philip jotted these lines: "How rich is a man who is free from security. / How rich is a man who is free from wealth."

CAROL OF THE SEEKERS

We have not come like Eastern kings,
With gifts upon the pommel lying.
Our hands are empty, and we came
Because we heard a Baby crying.

We have not come like questing knights,
With fiery swords and banners flying.
We heard a call and hurried here –
The call was like a Baby crying.

But we have come with open hearts
From places where the torch is dying.
We seek a manger and a cross
Because we heard a Baby crying.

CHRISTMAS 1939

"THE OLD ROAD TIRES ME"

The old road tires me
And the old stale sights,
And I must wander new ways
In search of sharp delights
With new streams and new hills
And smoke of other fires;
For a new road tempts me –
And the old road tires.

1940

This little poem opposes the patriotic nostalgia that ran through both Britain's war propaganda and the popular poetry of Philip's youth. Unlike Housman's Shropshire lad, he did not long for home, and, much as he loved the earth, he would never be wedded to one particular patch of ground. He had heard a call, and was ready to "wander new ways." But he could not have known how very far from his native Devon these ways would take him.

PLOUGHING

CHAPTER 2

Bruderhof members farming in Shropshire, England

It's time the soil was turned

So this new life began, with its new work. Philip laboured
with the men in the fields and vegetable gardens. In spring
the tractors ran day and night, ploughing, harrowing, and
seeding the spring wheat. Often, the whole community
would be called out before breakfast to help harvest
vegetables, which had to be picked early to remain fresh
for the farmers' market. In autumn, pitching the sheaves
into wagons and stacking them in a giant shock was a
communal event, as was the day the threshing machine
arrived on its round of all the local farms.

Philip loved it all – the seedtime and the harvest – and
his poems from this time reflect this newfound joy.

BREAKFAST SONG

Come let us to the fields away,
For who would eat must toil,
And there's no finer work for man,
Than tilling of the soil.

So let us take a merry plough,
And turn the mellow soil,
The land awaits and calls us now,
And who would eat must toil.

1940

THE PLOUGH

Now let us take a shining plough
And hitch a steady team,
For I have seen the kingfishers
Go flirting down the stream.
And sure the Spring is coming in –
It's time the soil was turned,
It's time the soil was harrowed down,
And the couch grass burned.

For we have waited for the chance
To turn a furrow clean,
And we have waited for the cry
Of peewits come to glean.
Now there's work from dawn 'til sunset,
For it's time the plough awoke,
And it's time the air was flavoured
With the couch fire smoke.

1940

FINGERPRINTS OF GOD

"Whenever I meet a man," he said,
"I look him low, I look him high,
To see if a certain gleam is born,
An inner light, deep in the eye,
The light of eyes that see in growing corn
Not only grain, not only golden bread,
But sweet and plain, the fingerprints of God.
What for a man is it, who cares
Only for harvest and the threshing feast,
Sees the reward before the growth of Love,
Who looks impatient at the slim green spears
That tremble under grey October skies
And scorns all but the ripened head?
God is not seen only at harvest time,
But he is here, in winter-sleeping sod,
And half his glory stands about our feet
In the low lines of green young growing wheat."

1940

EXPERIENCE — BEWILDERMENT

I have stood all day on sodden earth,
Beneath the heavy hand of weeping skies,
But golden fancies hammered at my brain,
An endless count of flying wonder-thoughts,
Pell-mell upon each other, and again
Forgotten, like the dance of dragonflies.

1940

The community happened to be close to several Royal Air Force bases – obvious targets for bombing raids. The men took turns serving as night watchman for the community.

THE END OF THE WATCH

There's a crowing of cocks, and a paling of stars,
And the hours of the watch are far on;
There's a flush in the east, and the pipe of a bird,
And the last of the starlight is gone.

The darkness thins out, and the new world appears.
The watchman prepares to depart.
Let him go to his rest with the sun on his face
And the splendour of stars in his heart.

1940

Now is the harvest of death

During the spring and early summer of 1940, while Philip
was planting and hoeing, Germany invaded Norway,
Denmark, Belgium, Luxembourg, and France. British
troops were rescued from Dunkirk, but only after thou-
sands had been killed or taken prisoner.

THE HOUR ON WHICH WE LOOK

Now is the harvest of Death,
Now the red scythe-blade of slaughter
Sweeps through the children of Eve.
We stand in a circle of silence,
The wings of the Reaper are hissing –
And what could our speaking achieve?

And we, as we stand in our silence,
Hear the laugh of the sower of fate,
Who scattered the seed in the hearts of the tribes,
And who reaps now the hate.

Only the music of a wild wind in the trees,
Or the rumble of thunder, the roar of the rain,
The shouting of demons who ride on the storm-winds of wrath
Can tell of the tempest that howls like a wolf on the plain;
Where the earth carried wheat, and the waters were sweet,
But now stink with the blood of the slain.

1940

Germany defeated France in just six weeks, and turned its eyes to its next target across the English Channel. Britain made preparations for the expected invasion.

Now that the people of England were rallying to fight for their country, they had little patience with war resisters. The government, however, provided tribunals to discern whether or not a conscientious objector to war was genuine in his request for alternative service or unconditional exemption.

Philip was called up before such a tribunal. On February 27, 1940, a local newspaper, the *Evening Advertiser,* reported on his case:

Swindon Man's "Love Beats All" Theme at Tribunal

Bruderhof Man's Conscience:
"A Christian Cannot Take Up Arms"

A probational member of the international community at the Bruderhof, Ashton Keynes, near Swindon, was an applicant for total exemption from military service before the South-Western Tribunal for Conscientious Objectors, at the University of Bristol yesterday. He was Philip Herbert Cootes Britts, and he was accompanied in court by several fellow members, bearded young fellows, who attracted considerable attention by reason of their unusual appearance.

Britts, in his written statement, applied for complete exemption from any form of war service because of his belief that a Christian cannot take up arms or use violence against his fellows; neither could he help others to do so. For the last five years there had been no question in his mind about that, he averred.

"In the spring of 1939," the statement proceeded, "I
decided to take part in organised pacifism and began to
promote my views among others. During the summer
I addressed the local Bible classes on this subject and set
about organising a group of the Peace Pledge Union in
Kingswood, Bristol. I acted as its secretary until I came
to the Bruderhof on 26 November. I cannot accept any
conditional exemption, and shall refuse any form of
alternative service."

The judge was satisfied that Philip's beliefs were genuine
and granted him an unconditional exemption.

It was no escape from conflict that Philip sought, but a
different struggle. "This is the meaning of brotherhood,"
he would write eight years later, "– not a haven of refuge,
but a joyous aggression against all wrong." What's more,
there would be no end to this battle, no decommissioning
and resting on one's laurels, no growing old and tepid.

THE OLD MEN WHO HAVE FORGOTTEN
WHAT TO DO WITH LIFE

They spoke of high adventure of a thousand mighty
    sorts –
Of bareback rides on foreign plains
And nights in foreign ports;
They laughed and cursed and downed their beer,
And all would talk and none would hear,
The bar was thick with noisy cheer
As the men sat drinking.

But one man sat in quiet, alone,
In one dim corner, sat and gazed.
He told no story, roared no laugh,
But sat and stared as one amazed.
The man sat thinking,
And ever in his mind there burned the thought,
Here is the poison – where the antidote?
Here is the evidence that men forget.
These have forgotten all the pith of Truth:
And most men with them, that I ever met,
In boasting age or swift careering youth,
Have missed the true adventure, missed the thrill
Of that great ride where they could drink their fill
Of wonder and of danger and of strife –
They have forgotten what to do with life!

These lusty men grow old
And gibber freely in their age
Stale stories of a hectic yesterday.

These lusty men grow old,
And all their hectic yesterdays
Are now like froth upon a glass of beer.

These lusty men grow old
And spend an idle eventide
Yarning about dead deeds with dying words,
And all their strength, their striving, and their fear
Is like a gust of wind, and all their feats
Like thistledown adrift in city streets.

But who can show strong men, as these,
The things that will abide,
The one Adventure, one great Quest,
From which there is no pause nor rest
When once the search is tried;
Where those who search and struggle
Win courage from defeat –
And, daring, drink the wells of Death,
And find the water sweet?

There is but one Adventure,
The seeking for the Truth,
One prize for those who find it –
Everlasting Youth.

When they were born, they knew it,
The men who sit here yet;
And every sunrise tells them, but always they forget.

1940

With Great Britain at war, what had become of the
Christian peace witness? In 1948, Philip would write:

> If a man who had been closely associated with Jesus
> of Nazareth were to revisit the world today, with no
> knowledge of the intervening history, it would seem
> strange to him that the numerous and widely-followed
> "Christian" churches are as perplexed and helpless in the
> face of the general dilemma as is the rest of humankind.
> He would have heard Jesus proclaiming a new way of
> love, a new kingdom of peace, and he would now find
> whole nations claiming to be his disciples and, not only
> living in violence, injustice, lying, and impurity equal to
> that of the pre-Christian world, but even using his name
> to bless and justify their wars.
>
> Where shall we look, and what have we to say in
> face of this confusion? . . . Is it not important that there
> should be some place in the world, however small,
> where people actually live in brotherhood and justice
> and peace – and that we give our lives to this cause?

To give their lives to this cause was precisely what Philip
and Joan decided to do. In the spring of 1940 they asked to
become members of the Bruderhof, making lifetime vows
of commitment.

"WHEN I HAVE GROWN"

When I have grown to strength of heart and mind,
Then let me still lie helpless on thy knee,
Still raise my empty hands towards thy face,
And let thy love, alone, smile out from me.

I am but earth, unless thou work in me
And make my earth bear fruit in every part.
Wound me, then, deeply, with thy plough of love,
And let there be no fallow in my heart.

1940

My family had joined the community shortly before
Philip and Joan came. We children felt an affinity for
him – he was quiet, thoughtful, awake to joy, and willing
to spend time with us. That fall, Philip wrote this story,
illustrated it with childlike black and white sketches, and
gave it to my younger brother, Anthony, and me for my
ninth birthday. I am no longer sure what prompted it,
but I may have asked him why there were flowers in the
woods in springtime, but not in the summer.

WHY AUTUMN COMES

Barbara had a big tabby cat, who was very old and very,
very wise. Nobody knew how old he was, because he
was already there when the community came to the
land.

Nobody knew how wise he was either, but they said
he was the Wisest-of-all-Cats. Indeed, he was able to
talk, and when Barbara was puzzled, he used to tell her
How-things-came-about stories.

One day when the brown and golden leaves were spinning down from the trees, and the Wisest-of-all-Cats was asleep by the stove, Barbara poked him with her finger and said, "All the leaves are falling off the trees, Cat, and there is a thick blanket of them on the ground. Why does it happen, and how did it come about?"

The Wisest-of-all-Cats stretched himself and said, "It's a story that goes back to the First Days, but I will tell you all about it."

In the days when the world was very young, a little girl was skipping over the grass, looking for flowers. And there were flowers everywhere.

The green carpet of the grass was spotted with many colours, and flowers grew together in little groups, in every possible place. Some grew in the sun, and some in the shade of rocks.

Presently the little girl saw a beautiful wood growing on the side of a hill. All kinds of trees grew in the wood, with leaves of different shades of green. She ran towards it saying, "I will pick flowers in the beautiful wood," and she walked between the trees and began to look for flowers. But though she looked very carefully, and walked a long way into the wood, she couldn't find a single flower, no, not one. So she put her arms around the stem of a tall beech tree, and said, "Why do no flowers grow under you, trees? There is plenty of room at your roots."

But the trees all whispered together in their highest branches, and she couldn't understand what they were saying. So she ran out of the wood to ask the flowers. And when she saw a poppy she bent over it and said, "Oh, Poppy, why don't you and the other flowers grow in the wood as well as in the fields?"

Poppy shook her head and said, "For myself, I must have the full sunshine. I cannot live under trees. But you could ask the flowers that grow in the shade of rocks why they can't grow in the shade of a wood."

So the little girl looked in shady places and found a shy white anemone and asked it, "Little flower, why don't you live in the wood?"

"I can't," said Anemone. "Trees are too greedy, they take *all* the food from the earth, and if I tried to live there, I should starve."

"Oh, what can we do about it? Is there nothing we can do?" cried the little girl.

And Anemone said, "You and I can do nothing, but if you really think we should live in the wood, you must ask the One-Who-Made-the-World. Perhaps he will make it possible. He can do everything."

"Yes, I will do that," said the little girl, and walked quietly away.

But the One-Who-Made-the-World had already heard her talking to the flower, and he began to make new laws, and miracles for the trees and the flowers.

When the little girl woke up next morning, she heard two little birds talking together at her window, and one said, "Tree has been told that he must give good food back to the earth because he takes so much, so that flowers can grow in the woods."

The little girl got up quickly when she heard this, and ran out to look at the wood. When she saw it she stared and stared. For yesterday the trees were green, but now all their leaves were brown and red and yellow. And every time the wind blew, some of the leaves fell off the trees, and floated spinning down to earth. Every day more leaves fell down, and soon there were no leaves at all left on the trees, but a thick scrunchy carpet on the ground. It made a dry rustling noise when you walked through it, and all the birds chatted away and said what lovely food it would be for the flowers. And in many ways it is the best of all food.

The trees stood all feathery and graceful against the clear sky, and the little girl thought they were even more lovely than before.

All through the winter she watched them, and grew to love them without their leaves. When the days grew warmer again, shy little flowers came up in the woods, primroses, violets, anemones, bluebells, one after the other, more and more.

But perhaps the best of all was the day when tiny new leaves appeared on all the trees. These new leaves were fresher and greener than ever before, and they were as soft as silk.

The Wisest-of-all-Cats ended his story and began to wash himself.

"Did it happen very long ago?" asked Barbara.

"Very, very long ago," said the cat, "before the Pyramids were built."

"Was it before you were born?" asked Barbara.

But the Wisest-of-all-Cats didn't answer.

SEPTEMBER 1940

I imagine Philip writing this story to the sound of air raid sirens. In July 1940 the Battle of Britain had begun in the skies over England and the Channel. Searchlights tracked enemy planes by night. Air raids – the anxious rush to shelters, the scramble for gas masks, and the noise of bombers overhead – interrupted both nights and days. And more hardship was to come for the community to which he and Joan had just pledged themselves.

One with thy brothers in the quest

When the war began, the British government started to
intern enemy nationals: all Germans and Austrians over
the age of sixteen were called before special tribunals.
Some were put into internment camps, though most were
released.

But as more of Europe fell and fears of German inva-
sion increased, the policy changed: early in the spring of
1940, more Germans were rounded up and interned. If the
English and German members of the Bruderhof wished to
continue living in brotherhood together they would have
to leave England.

But where to go? The community looked for months
for a place that would take them and allow them exemp-
tion from military service, freedom of religion, and the
right to educate their children as they saw fit. Finally, they
got word: thanks to the intercession of Mennonites, the
government of Paraguay agreed to accept the Bruderhof
on these terms. Fortunately, the Home Office granted
exit permits to all members of the community, even to
medical doctors who could have been a help at home in
Britain during the war.

A few lines Philip wrote later reflect what this moment
must have meant for him:

As pilgrims we must stand ready, with our boots on our
feet and our staffs in our hands, not tied to any earthly
possessions, or any particular geographical place, and
with no other loyalty than that to God and his kingdom.

In October 1940, the first group of members and their
children, eighty-one people, left for Paraguay aboard
the *Andalucia Star* ocean liner. These were dangerous
times for travel. While British cities were being bombed,
battleships, submarines, and aircraft were fighting for
supremacy in the Atlantic Ocean–England was under
siege. When we said goodbye to each other we did not
know whether we would meet on earth again.

Resettlement promised to be prohibitively expensive.
As the community continued to wind up its affairs,
a group of young men, including Philip, took jobs to
help raise funds. They found work with a government
program that had recently been started to reclaim aban-
doned agricultural land. Every arable acre was needed
to feed the island nation while the German blockade
prevented England from importing food. The young
men travelled by truck to the village of Malmesbury each
morning, where they dug drainage ditches and cleared
hedges, singing as they rode along. Bread and red beet
jam served as their lunch.

One morning Philip suggested they all help to write a
new song. Each worker offered a line and Philip pieced it
together.

THE SONG OF THE HEDGERS
AND DITCHERS

When the earth is sleeping,
When the fields are bare,
Only low wheat peeping
In the bitter air,
Forth we go at sunrise,
Through the frosty morn,
With our hooks and shovels
On our shoulders borne.

Deep we dig the ditches,
So that waters flow;
Low we lay the hedges,
So that shoots may grow;
Home we come at sunset,
Weary shoulders bent,
But the land will blossom
From the strength we spent.

1941

Meanwhile, the community continued the drawn-out process of emigration. The second large group sailed for Paraguay in February. On February 6, Philip wrote:

> On this, the eve of the departure of 158 of our people for Paraguay, leaving behind a group of about 70 souls in England, our hearts are full to choking. For we are more dear to each other than son to mother, or daughter to father.
>
> There is one gift of love we can give to each other before we part. That is that we, all of us, those who are going and those who are staying, pledge ourselves anew to the *one* way, the *one* fight, the *one* life. So that those who go may know that those behind have taken up the common task anew. And those who stay may know that those who go are bearing the common message.
>
> So let us pledge ourselves anew to God and to each other.

Philip began to keep a journal to record the last weeks at the Cotswold Bruderhof:

FEBRUARY 7, 1941

This morning 158 of our people left us on their way to Paraguay. They were all firm in the faith and dearer to us than flesh and blood. They left to carry the message of love and unity and peace in brotherhood, to a new land, far away. With these people, especially in the latter times, we had come to the deepest and most joyous experience of the unity of Christ. We were and are one folk, one people.

No words can describe the pain of parting with them. The hushed circle was a remnant facing an unknown future. We have all free-willingly stayed behind to carry on the task of the church in this country, so far as we are able, and to wind up the affairs of the community. What will happen, and how long a time will pass before we see them again?

SATURDAY, FEBRUARY 8

In our little circle, at suppertime, we sang with a new feeling the evening song, "The day thou gavest, Lord, is ended."* Particularly dear to us were the lines: "The sun that bids us rest is waking our brethren 'neath the western sky."

In the evening, the members met in the alcove of the dining room, and arranged for our people to move from the outer houses towards the centre, and also to see if it was possible to continue to have a night watchman. This we are doing and I am very glad, for the church must not sleep in times like this.

FRIDAY, FEBRUARY 14

This day we received the first letters from our people in Paraguay. It was such a joy to hear that all were safe and well, and the letter was very cheering for those who were to leave us this very day.

At four o'clock we gathered around the cars that were waiting to take them the first hop of their journey to Paraguay. It has happened so soon after saying farewell

---

* Words by John Ellerton, music by Clement C. Scholefield, published in Sir Arthur Sullivan's *Church Hymns with Tunes*, 1874.

to the others. Oh, that this might be the last parting we must make and that we may all be reunited. We ran and waved until the cars were out of sight, then turned back to the half-empty community.

I thought, when our people left, that we should care no more for the offerings of England, and indeed, on *that* day, we heard and could see no birds except the Phoenix. But although we find that part of our hearts have gone across the sea, the handwork of God in England is still sweet. So is the task for God that Jesus has called us to take up.

We long to be with our brothers who are in a land of blazing sun and flowers. But the chaste snowdrops comfort us, as do the modest English birds.

We have learned a new song which says something of this. It begins: "Morning has broken, like the first morning. Blackbird has spoken, like the first bird. . . ."*

SUNDAY, FEBRUARY 23

[We have] come to an agreement with the government department interested in the purchase of our community. After long negotiations, which have often been distasteful, we have agreed to sell at about 4,000 pounds less than we had hoped.

The dirtiness of the whole fight for property stands out in this transaction. Throughout all the meetings and discussions, agents, valuers, and prospective buyers were

---

* Words by Eleanor Farjeon, 1931, set to a traditional Scottish Gaelic tune, later popularised by the British singer Cat Stevens in a 1971 version.

continually engaged in "private talks" with someone
else. The agent who was trying to sell for us would have
a private talk with the valuer. The valuer would have a
private talk with the prospective buyer. The prospective
buyer would have a private talk with our agent. Each
one was out for his own ends. And some of them,
though not the government, were anxious to exploit the
position in which we were placed.

THURSDAY, FEBRUARY 27

Today we received a cable from South America saying
that our people had bought a large piece of land in
healthy, beautiful East Paraguay. This is near Asuncion
and a much better place to settle. We must try and raise
some money!

There is a break in his journal entries, and then:

MARCH 11, 1941

For many days I have been unable to write in this book
because of the clouds of evil that have blown over me. I
spoke in a members' meeting, in cold anger, and without
love or truth. For two days the help of my brothers did
not move my heart. This is all past now. The love that
was shown to me melted the ice in my heart.

During the week we received cables telling us of the
safe arrival of the big group in Rio de Janeiro and then in
Buenos Aires.

About 250 of our people have crossed the sea, in five
voyages, in these desperate times, and not one has been
lost. We can never be sufficiently thankful to God for
this.

THURSDAY, MARCH 13

Today we received a cable from Paraguay. It contained good and cheering news: "Health good, not dependent on further money . . . come immediately!"

FRIDAY, MARCH 14

A meeting of the members was called immediately after the midday meal. We had heard, this morning, that a ship would leave England for South America on Monday morning. We were offered places for twelve adults. No children could go, and all twelve places must be filled. If we did not use this ship, the seventy-seven places we were offered for April would not take all our people.

Our chief feeling was one of awe and thankfulness for the goodness of God. The news of this ship had come out of the blue and like a ready answer to our seeking. We felt clear that God meant us to join our brothers in Paraguay.

But how could we fill these twelve places? Who could we send? No one could be spared. It must be remembered how short the time was. The names had to be in that very day. We had to meet a completely unexpected upheaval in a few hours. If it was impossible, the impossible had to be done. . . . At last names were agreed upon [and Joan's and mine were among them].

Now arrangements had to be made for the carrying on of the work after these twelve had left. Joan was the only member familiar with the children's cooking; Buddug was to take her place, and Joan must try and pass on as much as she could to her, in the one day that was left. I was responsible for the cows, and fortunately on the previous day I had started turning the cows out during the day. In order to cut down the work, if the good weather held, we could leave all except the heavy milkers out at night as well.

Philip and Joan crossed the ocean safely on the *Empire Star,* which (like every other ship carrying Bruderhof immigrants to Paraguay during the war) was later sunk by the German navy. Philip penned the following poem aboard ship somewhere in mid-Atlantic.

THE QUEST

Tune: They All Were Looking for a King

To meet the challenge of the sun
Awake and gird thyself my soul,
Put forth upon the outward way
To seek the shining goal.

Go seek the land of brotherhood,
Go seek the city on the hill,
One love shall bind thee to all those
Who seek with heart and will.

And though the sun climbs up the sky
And hot salt sweat pour down thy face,
Turn not aside, for pause or shade,
Expect no resting place.

Fear not the sun shall beat thee down,
Though heart shall faint and limbs shall fail,
But look ahead with eager eyes
The far and fiery trail.

And joyful journey on until,
One with thy brothers in the quest,
Thou build the city on the hill
Where all shall find true rest.

1941

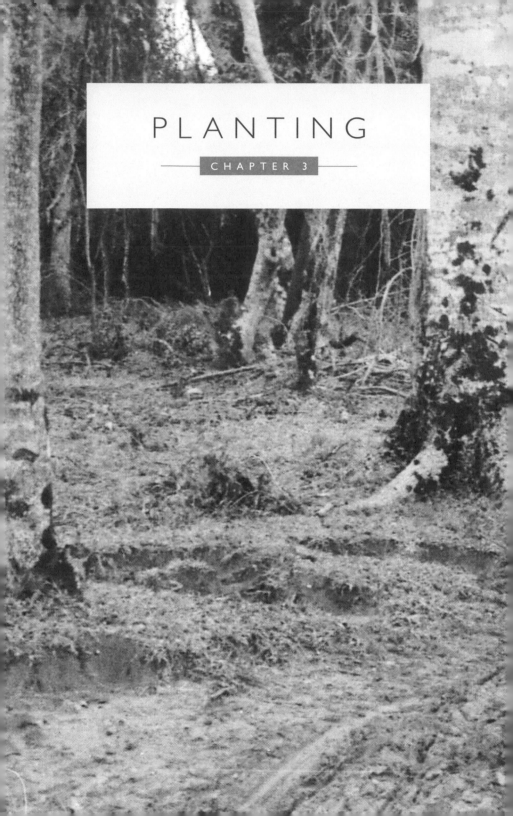

PLANTING

CHAPTER 3

Local mode of transportation in Paraguay, 1941

Not only the wonder of reaping

Philip and Joan had left England in the early spring of
the Northern Hemisphere, and arrived weeks later in
Paraguay's southern autumn. They joined the others
on the land that the community had bought: a place
named Primavera, "springtime" in Spanish. Several years
later, Philip would put together an information sheet for
prospective guests describing arrival in Paraguay:

> PARAGUAY is an undeveloped country, little touched
> by modern progress: conditions everywhere are
> primitive. . . .
>
> THE RIVER BOATS which take passengers bound
> for Primavera from Asunción to Puerto Rosario, are
> small and often overcrowded. The Paraguayan boats are
> slow and dirty. Two Argentine boats, which also make
> the journey, are better.
>
> THE ROAD that connects Rosario with Primavera,
> like all roads in the interior of Paraguay, is a rutted,
> sandy cart-track. . . . The usual transport is by light
> four-wheeled carts drawn by two horses. The journey
> by cart takes from twelve to twenty hours according to
> conditions and may be very dusty or very muddy.

THE CLIMATE is generally hot, summer temperatures rising above 100 degrees Fahrenheit in the shade. But from April to August, cold nights are frequent, occasionally with frost, but certainly chilly in contrast with the heat of the day.

PRIMAVERA. The community has been built out of the wilderness. Houses are primitive, mostly with thatched roofs, wooden or clay walls, and earthen floors. There is an abundance of dust in dry weather and mud in wet weather.

The community had to start from scratch, like the pioneers of North America. The neglected cattle ranch that the Bruderhof had bought was surrounded by twenty thousand acres of jungle and swamp. The men had to build quick shelters, dig wells by hand, tame cattle, and plough virgin land with oxen to prepare for sowing seed.

All the men and most of the women would rise at 4:30 a.m. and work for two hours before breakfast. It was too hot to work in the midday heat, so there was a pause from eleven to three. Philip would join the other men in the shade to peel *mandioca* (cassava) for the next day's three meals. At three the fieldwork resumed until sundown.

Philip worked with a team of young men to fell trees, which would be used as firewood and as timber for building. To provide water for the community, the same team took turns at the hand pump – a thousand strokes each, then a rest. It was heavy work; but one young man, a musician, pretended to be pumping an organ for music by Bach, and sang along to the rhythm.

"LET THERE BE NOT ONLY THE ROSES"

Let there be not only the roses,
Not only the buds of the day,
But the noon, and the hour that discloses
The full flower torn away:

Not only the bliss and the sweet
When the sun is soft and low,
But the weary aching of feet
Tired out by the harrow and hoe:

Not only the gazing and sighing
Where the heather stands thick on the moor,
But the lonely watch and the crying,
With hunger awake at the door:

Not only the anthems eternal,
Song without hurry or pause,
But the sweat and the stink and the screaming
Of circular saws –
Not only the mercy of dreaming,
But the labour and learning of laws:

Not only the wonder of reaping
The fruit that hangs red on the bough,
But the strain and the stagger of creeping
In the brown wake of the plough.

Let this be the way that I go,
And the life that I try,
My feet being firm in the field,
And my heart in the sky.

1941

WATER AT THE ROOTS

LABOURER'S EVE

With such exquisite beauty the day died:
We leaned upon our spades
And watched the colours deepen;
And it seemed the woods watched with us,
Every tree expectant, breathless,
While the beauty changed and grew.

Then a little wind passed by us, like a spirit:
It was reward enough for all the labour and the sweat.

And it was satisfying
To see the smoke of our couch fires
Drift over the valley
As the moon turned silver;
It was good to be weary
From heavy labour,
And to turn homeward, stumbling over the cluds in the
    dark,
And in our hearts the question, never quenched –
Why was there such a splendour in the sky?

1941

The community had been welcomed by other Europeans,
the German Mennonites. The general population, the
people known as Paraguayans, were a mix between the
Spanish conquistadors and indigenous Guarani tribes;
most of those who had not assimilated had been killed.
A small number of Aché Guarani had survived and, in
hiding, still lived by hunting and gathering as they had for
hundreds of years.

Now and then a rumour surfaced that someone
thought they might have seen an *indio* somewhere in an
unexplored jungle, not too far away. This was tantalising
news for the school children of Primavera, who were
intrigued by the possibility of meeting an Indian or, better
still, a whole family.

"IT IS NOT OFTEN HE IS SEEN"

It is not often he is seen,
Who haunts the virgin wood;
Only when one is miles away in dream,
Sometimes, on looking up, there is a man
Standing at the edge of the trees,
Staring with soft and lonely eyes
Towards the village.
Then with a little gesture that might mean
"Such things are not for me"
He turns and plunges in the forest gloom.

And village people, who are bold
To walk in the harmless glades on the forest fringe,
Have found, sometimes, a bunch of little flowers
That none of them has ever seen before –

They are the sweet white flowers that grow
Only in the depths of the forest, in the gloom,
Where the villagers never go.

AUGUST 16, 1941

People in the neighbourhood heard that there were doctors and nurses among the members of the community and began to come for help. But the "clinic" was only a small section of the first primitive shelter built for accommodation, and the medical staff had very little to work with.

One evening the community gathered under the trees after sunset. Darkness falls swiftly in the subtropics. A storm lantern hanging from a low branch illuminated the faces. One of the men reported on the war raging in Europe. Then from the tiny clinic nearby came the sound of a child crying in pain. Her Paraguayan family began to wail, a custom in the country. Mahranita was dying.

The community agonised with the little girl and her family, and wondered about their own future. They themselves had lost seven infants in that first year of living in the wilderness. Anxiety and a sense of foreboding threatened to erode the courage and joy that had upheld them so far. Backbreaking labour, the climate, disease, and desperately poor food and living conditions added to the burdens of each day, and fault-finding and despondency had been making life even more wearisome.

And yet, as Philip's poems from these months show, there was also a sense that God was still near the struggling community; and – as the poem of December 13 shows – a determination to fight rather than yield to despair.

Supper was over: we sat
Watching the eyes gleam in the lantern light,
While someone told us something of the wars.
     The Germans claim
A million Russians have been killed.
A million men are battered into blood.
A million hearts are stilled.
     And what is it to us, who live
       So far away?
And what is it to God, who made a million stars?

In the wooden building where our doctors work,
A child lay dying,
Cancer in the brain.
And on the stillness of our little night,
Her mother's voice struck, desperate and shrill,
Calling her daughter back from death:
     "Mahranita! Mahranita!"
Trapping the blood in our ears and hearts,
     "Mahranita! Mahranita!"
So that we all cried with her on the night,
     "Turn Death away! Turn Death away!"

And when she died, who was a stranger's daughter,
Our hearts plunged down in blackness, for a wing
Brushed cold across our forehead, snaky dark,
And now 'round every corner of our square,
Where every day the children play and sing,
We knew Death, vast and hungry, at our throat.

What is it, then, to God who gave the spark?

1941

FEAR

I have known fear,
   And sickness of heart –
Not the fear of men,
   But a fear apart
That poisons the breath
   (Not the fear of death
When the thunders start).
   Not evil to me do I fear

(I would drink the gall),
   But that someone is struck who is dear
When the bludgeons fall;
   And the judgement of God
Which I fear and must fall in the end,
In striking me down (which is just)
   Strikes also my friend –

I have cried in despair
To the skies at night:
   God, who art there
In glory and light,
   Check not thy hand,
Deal thy judgement to me,
   Who so arrogant stand
And will hear not nor see.

But one mercy I beg
From the fear in my heart:
   Deal thy judgement on me –
Let my friend stand apart.

1941

THE FIELD AND THE MOMENT

The shadows of three men sowing watermelons
Grew very long behind them as they crept down the
    field.
A pair of parrots flying homeward
Shouted noisily to them to look at the sky:
But they continued stooping and dibbling the seed in the
    earth.

In this way they grew a number more melons
And missed what was written in that particular sunset,
Which had never been written before
And, of course, will never be written again.

NOVEMBER 1, 1941

DISTRACTION

The wisdom of the prophet
And his words of gold
Surged around my brain –
And away they rolled;
Though I set my mind to hear them
They brushed at me and flew,
Because my spirit did not feel
The things the prophet knew.

The wisdom of the prophet
And his ringing words
Said less to my ears
Than the song of birds:
Because all the bird-wings
Beat about my ears
With sea winds and breakers
And loneliness and tears.

I went out from the prophet
And his drumming word,
Groping in the darkness,
Shaken and stirred:
For my spirit was full
Of the sad wild birds,
Of people grieving
Beyond all words.

I could not longer listen
To the prophet's words,
For my ears were filled
By the wings of birds:
Of weary living people
Beyond the weary sea,
Bleeding and crying,
Because they are not free.

NOVEMBER 2, 1941

"IN THIS STILLNESS"

In this stillness,
In this silence,
Speak the stars
And speaks the sky,
"Reconsider,
O my people,
All the things
You know me by.

"Honey-bee
And woods of orange,
Pineapple
And rice and maize,
Softest wings
Of sleep at night-time,
Strength for labour
Through the days.

"Not that you
Should probe too deeply,
Burning mind,
On mystery,
Not that you
Should strive to reach me,
Climbing by
Intensity.

"What have you
To offer to me?
What is it
You feel I ask?
Reconsider,
O my people,
What you see
To be your task.

"Not that you
Forever harp on
Things so clear
To me above –
Simple are my
Expectations.
All I ask
Is that you love.

"Love is clear
And Love is simple,
Quick to help
And slow to cease,
Love is Gratitude
And Patience,
Love is Kindness,
Love is Peace."

DECEMBER 4, 1941

"THAT MY WHITE LAMB"

That my white lamb is being carried off
In steel-like talons to the unknown hills
And is a lost speck only, in the sky –
That is not the chief thing;

Or that I did not have the strength or skill
To drive off the attacker, to defeat
Merciless claw and swift unerring beak
Or shattering wing;

But my fist is smashed and bloody
And my arm is a scarlet rag,
Showing I struck at the eagle –
And that is the chief thing.

DECEMBER 13, 1941

The next poem is based on Isaiah 26:13–19, the "Song of
Victory" or the "Song of Salvation," which the ancient
children of Israel sang after God helped them throw off
the yoke of their oppressors. It's not hard to see parallels
with the lot of the fledgling settlement in Paraguay.

A SONG OF ISAIAH

We have had other lords, O God,
Who held dominion in our heart,
But thou hast swept them all away
And in thy place they bear no part.

The gods are dead – they shall not live,
They have gone down, and shall not rise,
For thou hast swept their power away
And cast their glamour from our eyes.

Thy people labour in thy sight,
Like women in the pangs of birth,
But all our labour is for naught,
We bear no glory in the earth.

But though we die, in thee we live,
Nor can the earth hold down our trust,
Thy dew shall call us back to life,
Awake and sing who dwell in dust!

1941

"IF I RISE IN THE NIGHT"

If I rise in the night,
And step naked into the blackness
And the roaring storm,
Will thy abundant rain wash me,
Wash away some of this grime,
Making my soul cleaner?
And will it be done
Through the streams of thy rain,
Or because I cast away fear
And stepped from my tent to the storm
Unafraid?
Or will it be because I heard
A voice in my heart, urging
Be clean, be clean,
And obeyed?

If I rise in the dawn,
And climb slowly into the hill-top
With an empty heart,
Will thy exquisite sky fill me,
Fill with a wonder my heart,
Making the soul stronger?
And will it be done
Through thy colour and light,
Or because I sought and was sure of
The beauty that you would reveal
To my eyes?
Or will it be because you have seen
How bare is my heart, expecting
The sun, the sun,
To arise?

DECEMBER 25, 1941

Always attuned to the cycles of the natural world and their effect on farming, Philip was also able to draw spiritual lessons from them, as shown in the following poem.

WAIT FOR THE WEATHER

It's good to plough when the earth is soft
     And the furrows smoothly go;
When the tilth is fine and the weather fair,
     It is good to sow.

So when the earth is baked to brick
     And wind is dry and sun is bright,
It's better to bide at home and wait,
     And put your harness right.

It's better to wait your time, and make
     Good order for when you start.
Then all day long, when the time is right,
     Plough with a thankful heart.

CHRISTMAS 1941

"WHO ARE YOU, REMOTE YET PRESENT"

Who are you, remote yet present,
Somewhere above the tossing palm trees,
Between the storm and the stars,
In the unknowable darkness
Between us and the stars?

Or do the storm and stars and all the dark
Lie between us and you
Who wait, an eye and an intention
Beyond the hope and the fear?

I am the eye of the woman,
The hand of the man,
And the mouth of the children
Who stand, loving, around you.
I am the love they offer you,
While you stand peering into the storm
And see only a darkness and a shadow;
    I am here.

DECEMBER 31, 1941

WATER AT THE ROOTS

The community was expanding its activities. More space was needed to store the next year's harvest, and more housing as well. The original land purchase had included a small settlement – just two houses – two miles away from the original cluster of huts. Joan and Philip moved there, along with another couple. By Good Friday 1942, fifty people were living there. Philip brought thorns from an *espina de corona* (thorns of the crown) tree and wove them into a crown for a small table in the centre of the meeting room.

There was still rampant sickness in the community. The doctors did what they could, but the lack of proper housing and medical facilities made disease difficult to contain. The summer months had brought intense heat and humidity, and adults and children alike suffered from strep throat, whooping cough, croup, jaundice, malaria, and dysentery. The youngest children were particularly vulnerable. Emmi Christa Kleiner, the subject of the next poem, was a ten-month-old baby, and the second child in her family to die in Paraguay.

BURIAL OF EMMI CHRISTA

Not in fear and desperation,
But in stubborn, silent protest,
In the earth we laid our baby:
All the calm and tragic mothers,
All the broken-hearted maidens,
All the solemn-visaged brothers,
And we heaped the earth upon her
In a stubborn, silent protest.

Presently we turned and left her,
Lonely on the forest margin,
Turned and went once more to combat
With the Prince of Death and Darkness –
Not as they whose cause is hopeless,
But in certain expectation,
Fighting on towards the kingdom
And the overthrow of evil.

MAY 1942

It was around this time that the community began
to build a real hospital to serve the needs of its own
members and of its neighbours. Philip wrote a short
report as a fundraiser:

> We have three doctors supported by qualified nurses
> and midwives, a bacteriologist, and a dispensing
> chemist. This staff is the only medical help available for
> an area extending a two- or three-day journey in any
> direction. . . .
> The equipment and medicine were scarcely unpacked
> when the first operation had to be performed – on a
> young girl for acute appendicitis. . . .

The people are very grateful for the help that can
be given and show their thanks by bringing gifts of
oranges, eggs, homemade bread or cheese, or even
a live hen. One old lady often comes nine miles on
horseback with a dozen or so eggs tied in a cloth as a
necklace round her horse. The poorest come on foot,
often walking a whole day through the heat. Many have
horses or can borrow one. Many a mother can say, when
a baby comes with pneumonia, that her last child also
came as a baby with the same disease, and is now fat and
strong. Sometimes, however, a dangerous or fatal delay
in seeking help has been due to ignorance or poverty, or
fear that because they have no money they cannot ask
for help. . . .

One can often tell when a serious case is about to
arrive: one sees an oxcart in the distance, driven slowly,
preceded by a mounted messenger who clears the
road. One can never tell what such a cart may hold.
Sometimes it is just a mother who wants all her children
examined and treated for hookworm. More often it is a
tragedy: a man injured in a quarrel, with bullet or knife
wounds several days old.

THE HEALING MOON

Tune: When I Survey the Wondrous Cross

Above the forest rolls the moon
And banishes the pall of night,
She floods this weary darkened world
With soft and soothing streams of light.

Her light flows over scenes of war
Where reeking trenches mar the field,
But oh the bitter hearts of men,
Would they to her calm influence yield.

She touches with a silver wand
Grim slums and sordid city streets,
Her fingers cool seek out the heart
Where high the haunted tumult beats.

And where the wild untrodden woods
Hide savage acts of claw and tooth,
She looks into the burning eyes
Of nature fallen far from Truth.

Give praise to God, for sweet the moon
That tells his mercies never cease,
While we await the coming dawn
When Jesus comes to bring his peace.

MAY 1942

THE ONCE-WILD HORSES

When we were wild horses,
How we used to race across the turf,
Clutch of the wind more solid than
    the rocks that spun
  away, behind, beneath our feet,
Not knowing if the range ahead
Were cloud or mountain.

But now we lie in tame pastures,
And drink tap-water,
Chewing hay that is thrown over the fence.

It is not that we are halter-led, and bucket-fed,
It is not that we pull unwilling wheels,
That makes the sunlight pale, the air insipid.
It is only the remembrance and challenge of the turf,
It is only that we no longer gallop
Headlong towards cloud-mountains.

1942

On January 23, 1943, the date of the poem below and midsummer in the Southern Hemisphere, Philip and Joan welcomed their first child, Simon, into the world.

HARVEST LULLABY

We must wait at home, dear,
    Baby and I,
Until the blazing harvest sun
    Has left the sky.

Father is a fieldsman;
    When you were born
He started out to harvest in
    The shining corn.

You shall grow the corn, babe,
    When you are strong,
Working by your father's side
    The daylight long.

Tall and thick the corn stands,
    Golden and bright,
And we must wait for father's step
    Until tonight.

JANUARY 23, 1943

A fellow community member, Francis Beels, who worked with him on the land, later said, "Philip was continually writing notes – partly agricultural information, partly thoughts about God's purpose for us and all people. In his quiet way and with a smile, he occasionally said he was gathering material for a book to be called *Written in the Soil* and dedicated to his first son, Simon."

When Francis and his wife Sylvia had their first child later the same year, Philip wrote a poem for them too. The palm mentioned in it is a reference to an ancient legend about the flight of the Holy Family to Egypt: the tree is said to have provided them with shade and then bent low to offer its dates to the child Jesus.

"BABY IN MY ARMS I TOOK"

Baby in my arms I took,
Through the gentle night,
Tawny, tawny were the clouds,
By the moon alight.

And we found a golden tree,
All alone and old,
Standing in the tawny light,
Palm tree made of gold.

Golden palm tree, bend your head,
Tell my baby why
Here you stand all tawny-gold,
With your head so high.

Whispered then the golden palm,
Bending low and near,
"Long ago another Child
Found me standing here;

And He gave me leaves of gold,
Laughing in His glee,
Saying, 'When the babies come,
Speak to them of me.'"

SEPTEMBER 5, 1943

Bruderhof members farming at Primavera

CULTIVATING

CHAPTER 4

Here on earth, in your own land

The community's farmers and gardeners were working hard to improve the community's diet by experimenting. Philip's horticultural knowledge was invaluable in this wild country. Rice, green beans, maize, *mandioca*, and sweet potatoes grew successfully, and Philip experimented with wheat, pineapple, and grapefruit as well. Other endeavours were less successful: a sudden frost killed the thousand banana trees that he and his fellow workers had planted. In a report published in 1943, community members Sydney and Marjorie Hindley write:

> Harvesting is a tremendous task in this prolific land. Nearly all has to be done by hand, and each Monday is used specially for this work, leaving all jobs that can be left so that every possible man can help with the gathering in of the various crops. The maize, for instance, covers about twenty-six acres of land. Each man takes a row and goes from plant to plant, breaking off the cobs and loading them in a cart which takes them to the storehouse. Here, they are later stripped of their covering leaves, and then put through a little machine to break off the grains, ready for feeding to stock or grinding into flour. Rice is harvested with penknives

and threshed with flails; and millet, which makes good fodder, we harvest in a similar manner. Sunflowers are grown for their oil and for poultry food.

Mandioca is harvested like potatoes, and we gather sufficient each day for our requirements, which means a great deal, for we have fried *mandioca* each morning for breakfast, and invariably boiled or fried *mandioca* for dinner and supper. It is also fed to the oxen, horses, cows, pigs, and poultry.

Before the farmers could cultivate the land, trees had to be felled with axes and sections of jungle cleared; the forest soil was fertile, whereas the grassland was often swampy and the soil poor. Tree stumps were left in place and the patches of ground between cleared by hand with a large hoe in preparation for a few seeds of maize or watermelon.

Some of the trees were used to make hardwood crafts to be sold in the capital city, Asunción, which was beginning to play a larger part in the community's life. A few of the community's young people had gone to the city to study, and one of the men got a job there as a civil engineer; the money he earned was used to purchase needed supplies for Primavera.

In September 1942, the community had opened a little branch in a rented house in Asunción, staffed by a couple who served as house parents. Over the next years, members rotated in and out, working, studying, selling turned wooden bowls, and shopping for the communities.

And then a new opportunity arose. The United States had begun siphoning foreign aid money to Paraguay in the hope of winning support for the war. One of the programs funded by Washington was the Servicio Técnico Interamericano de Cooperación Agrícola (STICA), or Inter-American Technical Service for Agricultural Cooperation.

In June 1943, Philip travelled to STICA headquarters in Asunción to research suitable crops for Paraguay's climate. The following month, several of the Americans he had met there took him up on his invitation to visit the community at Primavera. Philip showed them the fields, the experimental gardens, and his notes. Soon realising that he knew more than they did about growing crops in Paraguay, the visitors offered him a job at their experimental farm and garden in Caacupé, a village not far from Asunción.

It was a difficult decision; the work would take him away from Joan and Simon. But the community needed the money, and he hoped to learn more about developing crops suitable for Paraguay. Philip accepted the offer.

The journey from Primavera to Caacupé, where Philip would spend most of the next two years, took several days. The thirty-five miles on horseback to the river port of Rosario took two days, or longer if the roads were bad. Then a full day on a riverboat to Asunción, where Philip would often stay over at the community's rented house. Then another thirty miles on a fairly good road to Caacupé.

Here he directed some of the 250 Paraguayan workers employed by the institute, conducting experiments in an attempt to improve the nutritional value of crops that could be grown in Paraguay. He had good success: one species of green bean in particular was promising. Philip and his team hoped that it would be taken up and grown by farmers throughout Paraguay, as a green vegetable supplement to the staple foods of maize, bananas, and *mandioca*. He also experimented with grasses for a better yield of milk, and with various strains of wheat and maize that could flourish in the subtropical climate.

At the STICA field stations where he worked, Philip got to know several North American colleagues who, like him, had wives and children far away. Talking with them, he began to realise that they were occupied by questions and issues similar to those that had spurred his own searching a few years before. In a world at war, for example, should they give their energies to defending the United States and the American way of life, or should they work for peace, and for the kingdom of God? If so, what would that mean?

Down the years a murmur runneth,
Bleeding hearts that wince in pain,
While the boasting politicians
Vaunt the claims of man in vain:

Building cities, stone on stubble,
Seeking safety in their might,
Till they grind the men to rubble
With their bombers of the night.

Through the earth there runs a challenge
Clearer than the trumpet call:
"Oh, forsake your ancient folly,
Build the brotherhood of all.

"Seek the city that God buildeth,
City of the heart and hand,
Not beyond the grave of shadow –
Here on earth, in your own land."

1944

As Philip continued to work in Caacupé, the farm he had overseen back home at Primavera was struggling. The summer of 1944 to 1945 was very hot and dry, sometimes 104 degrees Fahrenheit in the shade. A long drought dried up the waterholes in the pasture land. Daily the thirsty cattle were driven two or three miles to water. Attempts were made to dig new wells, but no water was found. The gardeners in Primavera managed to save the vegetables, but many other crops were lost.

"IN THE BRIGHT NOONTIDE"

In the bright noontide
Fadeth the rose,
Cometh and passeth
The wind on the grass;
Through all that changeth,
Fadeless, endureth,
One love unchanging,
Never to pass.

JUNE 1945

The community needed Philip's help – and Joan did too. Philip left Caacupé and returned home. Jessica, their second child, was born on January 25, 1945.

Among his other writings, Philip occasionally turned to translation, rendering in English portions of the writings of Eberhard Arnold. The following extract is one such translation; the second paragraph is Philip's addition.

Whenever a child is born it is something very mighty, something unbelievably great. An act of creation has taken place, in that a little soul is given to humankind from eternity.

A new little life is given into this world, which has in it something unique and original from the hand of God, and has before it a life, of length unknown to us, in which a new note should be sounded in praise of God, a new colour revealed in the infinite expression of God's love.

Therefore we cannot understand it if people think there is something regrettable in having to leave other work for the sake of new children. For us there is no lovelier work than the work for and with children.

The longest drought shall pass

Though home again at Primavera, Philip continued his horticultural work with STICA. Using twenty acres STICA rented from the community, he set up three experimental farms, on which he and other community members conducted their research. Over the following years he travelled to Asunción and Caacupé many times to report on his findings. His work was extensive, rigorous, and of lasting value: his research notes filled eight volumes.

Another trip came about because STICA asked Philip to visit the Instituto Agronômico in Campinas, Brazil, a well-known experimental station. He and a companion set out on February 12, 1945, in the hope of continuing his studies, raising funds for Primavera, and visiting a small community called Las Palmas. They returned home in April to find that rain was beginning to fall again – a cause for relief, as reflected by the next poem. Of course, it wasn't only the end of a dry spell: Philip's joy was just as much a reaction to the end of the war in Europe in May.

"THE LONGEST DROUGHT SHALL PASS"

The longest drought shall pass;
The heavens gather now.
New life for tree and grass,
Work for the plough.

On high in forest tops,
The eager bees do wing,
See how the mighty trees
Blossom and sing.

All life is joy again,
The longest drought shall pass,
Bringeth sweet drenching rain,
Life for the grass.

JUNE 1945

On August 6, the United States dropped the first atomic
bomb on Hiroshima, Japan, with devastating results; a
second bomb followed on August 9, destroying the city
of Nagasaki. On August 14, Japan surrendered. World
War II was over, and everyone was talking of peace. And
yet, the world had entered the nuclear age. What was
this "peace," which seemed to be built on anxiety? And
how could the wounds of the last war be healed?

Millions of people live in fear of another war. Perhaps
the vast majority of the citizens of the modern civilised
countries are in some way haunted by the fear that
sooner or later carnage will be let loose far more
horrible than the war so recently concluded.

It must seem a hopeless thing for an individual or a
group of people to oppose the stream of world affairs.
Yet there must be millions of thinking individuals, and
perhaps thousands of groups, who view the course of
civilisation with dismay.

"THERE IS A CALLING"

There is a calling in the ears of men –
A wind that whistles in the city street
Calling them back, to long-forgotten ways,
Blowing the sands of havoc round their feet.

There is a vision in the eyes of men –
Of fair wide fields, where gleams the honest plough,
Guided by hands of brotherhood and peace,
Far other than the hands that guide it now.

There is a struggle in the hearts of men –
A groping of the lonely in the fight,
Urging them on a road but dimly seen,
Towards faint music and a distant light.

O may that music swell, that light increase,
And hearts be strengthened in the inward strife,
That men may hear, and see, and struggle on,
Seek a new world, and find a truer life.

NOVEMBER 1946

Philip knew that his part in building the post-war
world lay in faithfulness to his calling and the people
of the Bruderhof. But he was committed to sharing his
experience with the wider world as well. Technological
advances had brought the atomic bomb, and modern
chemistry had made Hitler's death camps possible. But
there had been technological advances in agriculture
as well. If handled thoughtfully, this technology could
be life-giving. Using technology appropriately, Philip
believed, involved neither uncritical acceptance nor
rejection of genuine improvements. And it would be

impossible to find this balance and integration without considering other aspects of life.

To address his fellow farmers, Philip wrote an article for a farming magazine. His prescience in this essay is notable. Writing against the backdrop of the unfolding Green Revolution, whose accomplishments were being applauded in most quarters, Philip warned his readers to look past the impressive short-term benefits. "Nature will rebel," he warned, "and bring down the measure of subjection by such hard steps as erosion, sterility, and disease."

How Shall We Farm?

A short examination of farming trends and possible developments

A response to the "organic" school of agriculture

Within the last half century we have seen a revolution in agriculture, typified especially in the rising use of chemical fertilizers and powered machinery. The change has brought consequences both good and bad. The tractor and the fertilizer bag are really means of speeding up farming – the first of speeding up man's powers of cultivation, the second of speeding up nature's supply of nutrients to the crops. They were called into being through the increased pressure of machine-age life upon the land, to supply the ever-increasing demand for more food, more oils, more fibres, with dwindling manpower. This demand has been largely met, and could have been more nearly met but for the ruinous periods of destruction in two world wars. But a price is to pay. Where this speeding-up has been done rashly, as it has on millions of acres of land, retribution has followed swiftly, and good farming land that nature took millions of years to form has been worn out and lost in a generation.

All farming, even in its most primitive form, is necessarily an interference by man with the process of nature. As agriculture has developed, this disturbance of nature, this effort at control over nature has increased. Adam was charged with the double task to "subdue and replenish" the earth. If a graph could be plotted of the subjection of nature by man, it would show a line, rising slowly at first, through several thousand years, then abruptly and very steeply in the last few years. A graph of the replenishment of the earth by man would probably show a slow rise throughout the centuries, but instead of following the sharp rise of the line of subjection in modern times, would perhaps curve downwards. This in spite of the extensive use of fertilizers, because chemicals without humus do not give lasting or balanced replenishment.

Where will the lines go from now on? Obviously if the measure of subjection continues to rise, and the measure of replenishment falls, if the lines get farther apart, nature will rebel, and bring down the measure of subjection by such hard steps as erosion, sterility, and disease.

Here and there are signs that some people are awake to the trend of things, and alarmed at the possibilities. Notable are such men as Howard with his "Indore process" of composting, Pfeiffer with his "biodynamics," Faulkner with his *Plowman's Folly*.* A drive for sounder farming practice is represented by a section of the British landowner class, who have been vocal in the House of Lords, and from time to time evidence is submitted by scientists and technicians from Experiment Stations.

* Albert Howard (1873–1947), Ehrenfried Pfeiffer (1899–1961), and Edward H. Faulkner (1886–1964) were pioneers in organic farming methods.

The cause of good farming is soundly served by such careful studies as *Humus* by Waksman, and *Soil and the Microbe* by Waksman and Starkey. But these books, thorough and sound as they are, are highly technical. They leave a gap to be bridged between the scientist and the farmer.

A still greater gap exists between what the farmer knows to be right, and what a competitive economy forces him to do.

Experiment Stations supply the farmer with valuable fractions of knowledge, which he has to fit into his scheme of farming. The results of experiments, and the elaborate methods for determining the "statistical significance" of the results, are not above question. However carefully they are planned and executed, however often repeated, they cannot give an infallible verdict on the effect of a practice in the long run, or even an infallible prophecy of the effect of a practice in the next repetition of it under slightly different conditions. At best they can only give evidence that certain effects do recur within a finite margin of variation.

But if one makes claims for, or passes judgement on, technical matters without the *restraint* of these "cut and dried statistics," several human tendencies must be guarded against. One is the tendency to overgeneralise, leading either to a one-sided championing of one direction or the other, or, equally false, to the compromise of taking a "middle way," whereas the technical truth for each specific case may follow a line swinging from side to side within a channel formed by a series of correlations. In farming, as in life, isolated factors lose their significance – it is the correlation of things that matters. Another expression of overgeneralising is to "give a dog a bad name and hang him" – for example, to attribute the use of fertilizers to an "NPK mentality" and dismiss the subject.* Not that Howard is guilty of this in his "An Agricultural Testament," but his readers must beware of taking such a lazy step in their own thinking.

One must beware, too, of the error of dubious analogies, such as likening the fluctuations in human direction to the swing of a pendulum, or an ascending spiral. It is not true, for example, to say that the pendulum has reached the end of its swing in the direction of mechanised farming or scientific research, and must now swing back towards peasant husbandry, or "love of the land." This implies that mechanised farming and peasant husbandry are irreconcilable opposites, whereas there is much in both that can and should go forward together.

One must beware of attributing to any one factor effects caused by a number of factors. Thus soil fertility is *not* the basis of public health. It is one of many factors and, I think, a major one. But food by itself, however good, will not produce health. We have to cope with other factors such as climate, hygiene, moral and social habits, etc. Even if all the factors we can discover were made to contribute towards health, it would be fallacious to suppose a disease-free mankind. There are deeper causes of disease and death.

In the same way, organic farming, by itself, as an isolated factor, can never reach its full significance. It stands for the great truth that agriculture can never be stable and permanent until man learns *and* obeys the laws of fertility, the cycle that includes the decay of the old and the release of the new, or, to put it biblically, to "subdue and replenish."

* Howard's work is the story of "a Fall" in which the "serpent" is Baron Justus von Liebig, who showed that plants need only nitrogen, phosphorous, and potassium to grow. Howard called this the "NPK mentality" after the chemical symbols for those three elements.

But it can only realise its full meaning in the context of an organic life. Man's relationship to the land must be true and just, but this is only possible when his relationship to his fellow man is true and just and organic. This includes the relationship of all the activities of man, the relationship of industry with agriculture, of science with art, the relationship between the sexes, and above all the relationship between man's spiritual life and his material life.

One of the great tragedies of the modern world is the complete divorce of the city dwellers from nature and the land. Civilisation has become like the "fat white woman" who "walked through the fields in gloves."*

The decisive factor in the success of the farmer will be, ultimately, the love of farming. This love comes when we find, not in nature, but through and behind nature, that something which impels worship and service. Part of the glory of farming is that indescribable sensation that comes, perhaps rarely, when one walks through a field of alfalfa in the morning sun, when one smells earth after rain, or when one watches the ripples on a field of wheat; the sensation hinted at by the poet, when his

> Restless ploughman pauses, turns and wondering,
> Deep beneath his rustic habit, finds himself a king.

This love is fed by understanding, by knowledge. Without going the whole way with Leonardo da Vinci and his "perfect knowledge is perfect love," the more one knows of the mysteries of the earth the better one can love farming in the sense of giving one's service to it.

One of the best contributions of the school of organic farming to agriculture is this call for a genuine love of the land.

* The reference is to a poem by Frances Cornford: "To a Fat Lady Seen from the Train."

Our communities in England and Paraguay represent an effort to extend this love of the land, of organic farming, to all the other aspects of life, to industry, craftwork, education, and the daily relationship of man with man.

Sociologically, the position of our community in Paraguay is an interesting one. We find ourselves a group of modern people transported to a land that is still only at the initial stage of the machine age (i.e., before the sharp rise in our supposed graph of the subjection of nature). We find ourselves setting out to farm with a modern scientific outlook, but without modern scientific appliances. What implements we have are of the pre-machine-age type, pushed by hand or drawn by horses.

We are faced with the necessity of feeding ten people from every eight acres that we are able to cultivate or stock, including maize, beans, *mandioca* (the potato of Paraguay), peanuts, fruit, vegetables, milk, and eggs. We are unable to imitate the Chinese with their unlimited expenditure of labour to maintain fertility, because we are always short of manpower. For this reason meat plays an important part in the diet, being cheaply produced on the native range.

To maintain the fertility of our land we use green-manures, for which we have plenty of scope in our nine-month growing season, and two-year leys grazed by the dairy herd, combined in a five-field rotation. During the short winter, those fields that are empty are protected by leaving the summer cover crop on the surface as a mulch, or by disking in rye, to be lightly grazed and ploughed under for green-manure.

We do not use fertilizers because they are too expensive, but believe we could advantageously use bone meal and cottonseed meal if they were economically obtainable. In the same way we would welcome the chance to use tractors if we had the money to buy them, which we have not. We do not, with Faulkner, reject the use of the plough. Although we believe there is such a thing as over-ploughing, we still believe in "the useful plough," providing one never ploughs without turning under organic matter, and never leaves the ploughed land naked to the weather in this climate of heavy rain.

We have only been tilling the land here for five years, but with the number of people supported per acre, and two crops per year, the demands on it have been heavy and are increasing. We are therefore vitally interested in the maintenance of fertility.

But just as we do not believe that organic farming can find its full meaning outside the context of the whole of life, neither do we believe that an organic society can exist for itself, or have its only significance for the small group of people who are living it.

One of two things must happen. Either man will decline, through war, famine, disease, and the falling birth rate – and the recent progress of science leads one to believe that this decline may be imminent and rapid, and accompanied by obvious horrors – or we must learn to live peaceably together, in a society where the demand for wealth or position, ease or comfort, is supplanted by the just sharing of everything, and a free giving of strength and brains in service, not of self, but of the whole.

We do try to farm organically, but we see this as only a part of an organic life, and existing in the context of a search for truth along the whole line. This gives rise to social justice as brotherhood, to economic justice as community of goods. We see these conditions as the necessary basis for a true attitude towards the land and towards work. Therefore our door is always open to all people who wish to seek a new way with us.

To the question, "How shall we farm?" must be added the question, "How shall we live?"

The following list was found in one of Philip's notebooks. Perhaps he meant it for publication, or as the outline of an essay he wished to develop someday.

Definition of a "Good Farmer"

A good farmer is one who:

1. Realises that his farm is an organic unit in which all the organs must function in cooperation and reciprocation.

2. Realises that the fertility of the soil is the life-blood of his farm and that this fertility is not static, but is a dynamic and perishable balance.

3. Realises that humus is the mainspring of fertility.

4. Realises that for each part of the farm there is a best natural use of the land, and conforms to it as far as possible.

5. Realises that climate is the most powerful single factor affecting crop production; that it cannot be controlled, and should not be fought against, but cooperated with.

6. Fights insects and diseases firstly by prevention and uses poison sprays, dusts, etc., with caution and reluctance.

7. Realises that grass is the earth's most important crop, takes care of his permanent pastures and uses temporary pastures to protect and replenish his soil.

8. Realises the importance of the genetic constitution of his plants and animals, and makes use of breeding to improve quality.

9. Has the energy, tenacity, and organising ability to keep the farm clean and tidy, and to keep clear records.

10. Realises that he knows next to nothing of all that there is to know, that he is dealing with eternal laws which he did not make and cannot alter, and that the most brilliant achievements of human knowledge are simply the closest obedience to these laws.

Philip's agricultural work and writing, however, did not prevent him from continuing to produce poetry – poetry was for him a necessary ingredient in life.

NIGHTFALL

The sun drops suddenly behind the hill,
I leave the desk, go out to watch the sky deepen,
Head weary with the day-long tap of thoughts;
Swiftly the fields darken.

A tree stands etched against the glowing West,
The trivial tinkle of the day recedes,
I feel the great earth turning, turning . . .
The birds are silent.

Only a five-ton truck, with headlights blazing,
Screams noisily up the long, dark hill,
Man too busy to heed the coming of the night;
A star watches.

CAACUPÉ, MARCH 1946

THE FOREST OF LIFE

(It is dangerous to seek tranquility)

Treetops tossing as the wind stamps by,
Leaves all a-chatter with a rush of song,
Wild birds swinging in a reeling sky,
Fierce is the wind and his feet are strong.

Below and away from the feet that pound,
Hushed is the glade, and dim and cool,
Pale flower-clusters star the ground;
Light on the edge of the forest pool.

Grey-brown shadows in the soft green shade,
Silently glide the deer to drink;
Tree-ferns tremble in the air afraid:
Crouches a tiger at the brink.

Rest and peace in the glades retreat –
Red death lurking where the leaves are long.
Treetops bowing to the wind's rough feet,
Birds all a-clamour with a clash of song.

AUGUST 1946

CULTIVATING

Where are now the roses of the land?

Despite his ongoing visits to Asunción and Caacupé,
Philip was now based back at Primavera and was able to
be present for important events in the life of the commu-
nity. He was there for a wedding celebration in October
1946; the bride was German, the groom English – a testi-
mony to the possibility of peace between nations recently
at war. In the following poem, which he penned for the
young couple, "May" is hawthorn.

AND THE TWAIN SHALL BE ONE

When morning flushed the hedgerow,
Bowed down with May in flower,
I felt the hidden challenge
Of Beauty as a Power:
And then it was your word, your look,
That woke and filled the hour.

Now, in the bright of noonday,
When strength is at the peak,
And life runs strong to labour,
With many things to seek –
For Truth to guide and Love to speed,
I wait to hear you speak.

And who can tell what battles
Shall fill the hard-fought day?
But stay, dear heart, beside me,
Along the unknown way:
That we may watch together still
The sunset on the May.

OCTOBER 1946

The community had grown steadily; by the end of 1946,
there were 466 people living together in Paraguay. And
on January 5, 1947, one more was added: Philip and Joan's
third child, a little girl whom they named Marion.

CULTIVATING

SONNET I

How often do we miss the fainter note
Or fail to see the more exquisite hue,
Blind to the tiny streamlet at our feet,
Eyes fixed upon some other, further view.
What chimes of harmonies escape our ears,
How many rainbows must elude our sight,
We see a field but do not see the grass,
Each blade a miracle of shade and light.
How then to keep the greater end in eye
And watch the sunlight on the distant peak,
And yet not tread on any leaf of love,
Nor miss a word the eager children speak?
Ah! what demand upon the narrow heart,
To seek the whole, yet not ignore the part!

1947

"That's Philip," one of his close friends, Chris Caine, later said of this poem. "His poetic and spiritual outlook on life was such a wide thing, so wide and deep. He was a quiet man; he didn't easily come to words. Sometimes, when you asked him a question, you wondered whether he had heard you because he didn't jump with an immediate answer."

Children loved Philip because he joined their games. He took time to talk with them and tell them interesting things about plants and nature. They liked his wide-brimmed hat, his Wellington boots, and his big white horse. When he made his rounds of the arable fields, he would even let them have rides on his horse.

The community hoped to be able to bring in other children too. During the war, everyone at Primavera had tried to follow the news as much as possible. They thought of their home countries, relatives, and friends. After the war, reports came in of thousands of refugees, including many orphans, and their hunger and desperate poverty.

The community tried to find a way to bring some of the orphans to Paraguay, sending representatives to Germany to negotiate. These men made good progress, obtaining provisional agreement from the German government and identifying sixty children who needed homes. In anticipation, the community began to build a brand new village. They cleared one hundred acres at a spot called Ibaté, three miles from the other communities, and built simple houses.

But the building project was soon interrupted. On March 10, 1947, Primavera received a cable from Germany: the government would not permit the children to leave. And that same week, civil war broke out between the two political parties of Paraguay. Under the terms of their immigration, Bruderhof members were exempt from military service, and they were determined not to take sides in the conflict. But that didn't make them immune to its effects. As the battle front moved back and forth through Primavera over the next six months, the soldiers repeatedly demanded cattle, horses, and wagons – a dangerous, and compromising, situation for a group of pacifists. In the end, they chose the most peaceful solution: they would not give the troops support, but did not hinder or retaliate when goods were taken.

Community member Hans Meier later wrote, "We experienced quite a number of very difficult and hectic moments, and Philip, with his quietness and calm, was very helpful at such times. I remember one afternoon when Philip came to my hut followed by a soldier with a loaded rifle. We both represented our attitude firmly and calmly. We were arrested and led away. It was only for a short time though, and what a joy when we returned home!"

POETS AND WAR

We may find roses in some sullen place,
Down hunger-bitten ways, where grey rocks stand.
They may be soothing to the tortured eye,
And yet the belly makes
A fiercer and an unallayed demand.

The poets tend the roses, and they blow
Some flowers of solace for the writhing mind,
But it takes more than this to grow the corn
Shall satisfy mankind.

We scorn the roses and for bread
We eat the glittering poison sand,
Then turn and dash each other on the rocks,
Strike flame, that fills the valley, blood and smoke.

Nor sweat nor tears
Can quench that searing flame, nothing but blood,
And when there's blood enough,
May rise a small green spear and tremble in the air:
But where are now the roses of the land?

1947

Finding the source-water

Philip had been corresponding with people in the
United States since 1946, in part through the Bruderhof's
longstanding ties to the United States Fellowship of
Reconciliation, an organisation founded in 1915 to find
nonviolent alternatives to war. Now Primavera began
to receive more letters, and even the occasional group
of visitors, from North America. After some guests had
arrived totally unprepared for the primitive conditions,
Philip created an information sheet for future visitors.

> The person coming to stay at Primavera must prepare
> himself for a series of discomforts. From Asunción
> onwards: a twelve- to fifteen-hour journey on a crowded
> and dirty boat; a scramble up the river bank into a rough
> "buckboard" cart; a day and a half of bumping through
> dust or mud and water; and a primitive hut at the end
> of the journey to live in as long as he stays. He must be
> prepared for plain food and hard work; to be soaked
> with sweat in the heat of the day and to shiver when the
> southern wind blows; to be covered with clinging dust,
> or be up to the ankles in mud; to be bitten by mosqui-
> toes, horseflies, and midges; to bathe in a bowl of water,
> and to sleep on a sack filled with straw on a bed made of
> boards. . . . Remember that the nearest shop is reached

by a four hours' walk (and then you have to come back), and walking is strenuous in Paraguay.

On April 8, 1947, in spite of some strange sores in his mouth – likely the first symptoms of a fungal disease he had unknowingly contracted while on a trip to Brazil for STICA two years earlier – Philip met with a group of guests from the United States. He said to them:

> Let us recognise how godless our times are, and how far we all are from God. Nothing tells us this more clearly than the torn and divided state of humanity, in mutually hostile and divided camps. Let us bear in mind that dreadful things are still happening: the bloody fights in Palestine and India, the cold, slow murder of the poor in Europe, the civil war in our own land, the increasing expenditure for armaments, the distrust and suspicion between the nations. What must happen? What must we do?
>
> We need people who are aglow with the fire of love to proclaim the judgement of God to the leaders and the nations. We need prophetic criers in the desert, to warn people to repent. We need people who live love not only with words, but also with deeds. We need people who have received such certainty and clarity from God that they recognise and expose evil, whatever form or disguise it may take, as that which destroys life. We need people who absolutely renounce all evil, in that they live utterly for the good. We need people who are ready to suffer mockery, imprisonment, brutality, or even death for the sake of love and justice, both in their own nation and among all people. We need people who quite truly, quite sincerely, and quite simply serve peace.

Even Philip's friends didn't know how many poems he
wrote, or what an important part of his life they were.
Still, once in a while he would share a poem, like the
one on the next page. Marianne Zimmermann, an avid
musician and occasional composer, later remembered the
occasion:

Our first Primavera dining room was a hut in a wood of
tall trees. Supper was over and I was leaving. It was pitch
black outside. The only light in the wood was a little
lantern hanging high in a palm tree to help the people
find their way home through the dark trees. Philip stood
in the lantern light, waved to me quite shyly – that is
how he was – and said, "I want to show you something.
Can you help me?" He pulled a small piece of crumpled
paper out of his shirt pocket. It was covered with dust
stains and looked as if he had written a few lines while
out in the fields. "I had to make a poem. Could you
perhaps see if it can be used somehow, if you can do
something with it?"

I read the poem immediately by the light of the
lantern. It struck a chord. I took the poem to Sylvia.
She, too, was inspired and wrote a beautiful tune by
morning. I added a setting and we showed it to Philip.
He was happy.

SONG FOR THE PRESENT DAY

He is speaking to the North, "O come!"
He is calling to the South, "Withhold no more!"
Come, O come, to where the King is calling,
Sending out a wind to wake the sleepers and the poor.

There is nothing that can bar your way,
Though the breaking may be blood upon the sand.
Lift your hearts, for hark! the wind is calling,
Breaking down the barriers however high they stand.

There are rivers running strong between,
There are watches where the stars are never still,
Come, though, come, to where the King is calling,
Calling for a people in a city on a hill.

In the tumult of a world of steel,
There's a whisper of a wind upon the street.
Rise, and come, though long and hard the journey,
Yonder is the city where the South and North shall meet.

1947

On the first of May the community celebrated the harvest with a festival. Philip gave a report on the arable and garden yield and concluded with the words:

> The more a community becomes divorced from the simplicity and faith of a rural life, the greater danger it is in of losing inner stability. One sees this so plainly in the world today, where the trend to industrialisation is proceeding more intensively than ever.

In addition to the sores in his mouth, Philip was now also suffering from stomach problems. This was not unusual in the tropical climate: everyone dealt with parasites at some point, so no one was particularly worried. The doctors tried to help, but the medication failed to clear up the disease. Philip continued his work.

Philip's humour popped up from time to time – often unexpectedly. He enjoyed making comical rhymes and verses for special occasions. On July 14, the community celebrated a young couple's engagement. Several young bachelors recited this ditty Philip had written, much to everyone's merriment.

THE BACHELOR'S LAMENT

We, the remnant, paying our dues to all this jollity
Would say a solemn word to our lost friend.
Before him now a new life stands,
He'll comb his hair and wash his hands,
He'll wipe his feet upon the mat,
And on a nail hang up his hat.
The usual things that young men do
Will definitely be taboo.
No more will he lie down so carefree, sweet –

The natural way, the way the young men sleep.
He'll take his boots off first and wash his feet.
Perhaps he'll even have to brush his teeth!
No longer will he stand around the stove
After the communal meeting,
Talking of weighty things from man to man,
But he will have to hurry meekly home
To fetch hot water or get into it.
Then on some stool, sipping a little tea,
He'll talk about how nice supper was,
Of how he'll plant a rosebush by the door,
And how he'll try to titivate the floor
Some midday hour.

But then, alas, such is the way of life,
A moment's weakness and a maiden's glance,
Man forgets all and takes himself a wife –
If he has luck enough to get the chance!

New families were forming and the community was
growing, so the members decided to occupy the newly-
built children's village at Ibaté. This new settlement
would need a pastor. The community met, and Philip was
chosen. He said he felt too young and inexperienced for
the task, but agreed to serve.

"THE SMALL PATH"

The small path wound between green barriers,
Contorted tree, and tangled undergrowth;
And a small path in my inner mind
Was winding through the tangle of ideas,
Trying to lead to a place of more meaning.

There came the moment when the leaf fell from the
    tree.
As I watched it twirling slowly earthwards
The talk of my companions faded from my awareness.

There is a voice which speaks to us
Within, from Without:
And when this voice is not in the voices of our
    companions,
At any moment we can be essentially alone.

Though my feet continued down the small path
    between the tangles,
Mind joined spirit, alone, on the other path,
Heeding a voice, not of words but water.

If any revelation came, it is no more remembered,
And the talk of the others led to no fundamental
    discovery:
But I had been drinking from a far fountain.

At some other time, perhaps I shall remember the
    meaning,
And be able to say something of it,
That we can find again the source-water,
Not alone, but together.

1947

HARVESTING

CHAPTER 5

Gardening at
Primavera

Something less visible than the atom

The call to be a pastor and leader seems to have marked a turning point for Philip: ideas and projects came thick and fast, and he wrote and spoke on many topics. Notebooks labelled for "Soil Preparation, Cultivation" or "Planting Rates and Methods" are filled instead with Bible passages, drafts of poems, and notes for essays and sermons. He worked on an English songbook and on a translation of an early Anabaptist confession of faith by Peter Riedemann. It was around this time that Philip wrote the essay "The Essential Conflict," which contains an idea he explored more than once, even in his agricultural observations: the important distinction between knowledge and wisdom. This theme echoed throughout the troubled times. As T. S. Eliot asks in "Choruses from The Rock": "Where is the Life we have lost in living? / Where is the wisdom we have lost in knowledge? / Where is the knowledge we have lost in information?"

The Essential Conflict

. . . The highest faith that can be given to man is the certainty of the ultimate victory of life over death. Before our eyes we see the alternating triumphs of life and death in nature, but the certainty of the ultimate victory of life has no outward proof. Everything on the earth passes away and is replaced by new life. We cannot know whether the starry universe is either infinite or eternal. The certainty of the victory of life can only be experienced within, by the voice of eternity, by the inspiration of the eternal One who is Life, saying in our hearts the undeniable I AM.

One aspect of the essential conflict between life and death takes the subtle form of the conflict between worldly knowledge and simple truth. Knowledge appears so powerful, so virile, that man sees in it an attribute of life and pursues it as one of his greatest hopes. Knowledge thrives and multiplies. Knowledge of one thing leads to another until a mighty apparatus is built up which apparently brings the whole creation under the power of man.

It has been seen and said by wise men in many ages that all this is vanity. Never did it need saying so much as today. With the harnessing of atomic energy as the latest triumph of knowledge, the potentialities for destruction are so vast and so imminent that a climax in human history is approaching out of all proportion to national or racial climaxes.

Not that knowledge serves only destruction, nor is technical knowledge the only knowledge which has been set up as a god. Religion has been clothed with many veils of knowledge: philosophy, psychology, sociology, and the like. And these are delightful to the mind, and all bring their own reward. But just these regalia of human knowledge so often hide divine truth. Truth that is simple and direct is surrounded by a maze of human speculation, and we wander interminably through the maze, admiring the roses, and not finding our way to the fountain of life-giving water in the centre.

When we attain to seeing that all creation and all
knowledge is a battleground between the ultimate
forces of life and death, or good and evil, in which we
stand free to give our lives to one or the other, then all
knowledge is valued only as a path which leads to the
forces of life.

This is the dilemma of the scientists who sincerely
feel that their quest of knowledge is a quest of truth and
therefore good. They do not realise that knowledge as
such is an instrument which can be used by either of the
two spiritual powers, that the final result of knowledge
is determined by the spirit it serves, and that it will serve
the spirit into whose hands we place it.

Before we seek or employ more knowledge then, it
is vital that we first acquire that knowledge which will
teach us to see the universal conflict and to distinguish
between the opposing spirits, and our first task is to
place ourselves with all our strength and faculties on the
side of life against death. Only when we take our stand
each day anew in this one essential conflict can we know
that our knowledge is serving life and not death. . . .

Despite being far from Europe and North America, Philip
did his best to keep abreast of events and topics. In a talk
to the community, he said:

In this faith we must turn away from the worldly
conception that man is the initiator and God the
responder; that we, by our religious efforts, can set
something in motion which God must obey in response.
To believe that by an effort of will we can mount nearer
to God or add one cubit to our stature is as unchristian
as the belief (which Karl Barth proclaimed at the
Amsterdam World Council of Churches) that we have
no task as Christians for the mundane affairs of this

world. Both beliefs have the same root – the spiritual
climbing of man to God – and produce very much the
same confusion as the ancient attempt to build the tower
of Babel.

Perhaps it was such theology Philip had in mind in this
humorous little reflection:

There once was a farmer who owned a large farm in
which many people worked. To the people he entrusted
the care and management of the fields, woods, streams,
and buildings and charged them to produce many
goodly fruits. One day he walked among them and gave
them practical instructions about how they should work.

After he had gone they began arguing among them-
selves as to what he had meant. Instead of hoeing the
crops they leaned on their hoes and held long discourses.
His instructions about hoeing had been simple – they
were to keep the crops free of weeds and to cultivate
the soil. But in their discourses they sought to improve
on this by classifying the weeds into which were most
dangerous and which could be allowed in certain places.
They discussed whether the weeds should be cut with
a sharp, glancing blow or whether they should be lifted
with the corner of the hoe blade. They produced long
theories on what was a weed and what, under certain
circumstances, could be termed a useful plant. They
measured the growth of the weeds, and finding it more
rapid than the growth of the crop, after many discus-
sions they decided that it was more profitable to let the
weeds grow than the crop plants.

By this time, certainly, the weeds had almost
smothered the crop, and one could only find a few
spindly plants here and there. The hoers, however, had
now learnt a great deal about weeds and the theory of

hoeing, and were able to prove to themselves, and to many newcomers, that the farmer saw all green plants as valuable, and those that were easiest to grow were obviously the best, and that if one only allowed the weeds to mature, they would produce fruits quite satisfactory to all concerned.

Theology has provided us with armour, thick and strong, to protect us against any sharp arrows of the spirit which are aimed at pricking us into any practical Christian action. . . . A theologian, after years of careful study, can produce a book which will give a most minute examination and explanation of something which Jesus said in a few words. But whereas the few words of Jesus are a direct and pointed challenge to some very definite line of action, the many pages of the theologian are an attempt to explain what Jesus meant, which usually ends by obscuring the issue or offering so many alternatives that action is effectively blocked.

A theologian is like an armadillo.

The civil war came to an end in August 1947. For the last several months of the war, the community had been effectively cut off from the outside world, unable to get to Asunción to sell goods and buy food; they had been living entirely off what they produced, and for several weeks had been forced to ration food. Now the turned bowls and candlesticks could once again be sold in Asunción and new supplies brought in, and Philip travelled to the city as well.

But by October the next danger loomed. Huge swarms of ravenous locusts – more and greater swarms than ever before – flew in and covered all the crops. When this news reached Philip, he was able to buy two flame throwers and some pesticide to send back to help in the battle against the infestation.

These worked against the locusts when they were young, but as they grew, different methods were needed, which required as many people as possible to help out. Fritz Kleiner, a community member, organised the digging of a half mile of trenches to prevent the locusts, which were still too young to fly, from reaching the fields of crops. Philip returned to help with this work in mid-November, and he encouraged the beleaguered workers:

> In the face of the strain of tasks beyond our strength, we must turn inwards to the source of strength. If we measure our human strength against the work which we see immediately ahead, we shall feel hopeless, and if we tackle it in our human strength, we shall be frustrated. Indeed, insofar as each one of us seeks to live a brotherly life in our own strength, he either falls into torpor or exasperation. There is no healthier lesson we can learn than our own limitations, provided this is accompanied by a resignation of our own strength and a turning to the strength of God. The wheel of community will fly apart unless it is spoked to the centre, and we are placing ourselves in danger whenever we fail to recognise this, whenever we go rushing onwards without taking time to turn inwards.

On another occasion Philip said:

> Good work and hard work belong to a brotherly and manly way of life. If we live for God, nothing we can do is too hard or too good. The work we do expresses the spirit in which we live. . . . But it is never as important as to sit at the feet of the Master, and to hear his words. Yet we must make sure that we are sitting at the feet of the Master, and not some psychic altar of our own.

Fritz Kleiner was a blacksmith by trade, and he and Philip had much in common. Both loved music, wrote poetry, and wanted to devote their strength and their lives to the kingdom of God. Fritz and his wife, Martha, had lost two little children within the first year at Primavera. One of them was Emmi Christa (see the poem on page 64).

In early December, Fritz was in the turnery making the base of an Advent wreath on the lathe, when a large piece of wood flew off and hit his forehead. Fritz's injury was life-threatening. Philip sat at his bedside for many hours.

A PROMISE

I hate the silent coming in
Of the cold and bitter tide,
So calm and so remorseless
The salt sea waters ride,
And when the sky is sodden
With heavy clouds and low,
I hate the coming of the tide,
So merciless and slow.

And yet if you were standing there
Alone on the sodden sand,
And in your eyes the helplessness
Of your unaided hand —
I would come and stand beside you,
That you might face with me,
The sorrow of the darkened sky,
The menace of the sea.

1947

Fritz died on December 3, 1947. To Philip, it must have been a devastating blow: apart from their affinity for poetry, Fritz and Philip were both young fathers. Of course, no one could have guessed that fourteen months later, Philip himself would succumb to the deadly fungal disease that, though still undiagnosed, was causing him chronic discomfort.

How does one go on and celebrate Christmas after the loss of such a close friend? If anything, the season took on an even deeper significance for Philip, who wrote the following reflection.

"STARS WATCHING AS THE EARTH SPINS"

Stars watching as the earth spins,
Part of the endless rhythm, day and night,
And month and year and cycles of many centuries,
Ice age, stone age, iron age, atomic age.

And one star over Bethlehem,
New yet ageless,
Starlight in a stable, and a newborn babe,
The first new man, but born of the beginning,
Origin and means and fulfilment.

The Word, the I AM,
Cutting across the ages.
Heaven and earth shall pass away,
But My Word shall not pass away.

In the heart of each man
A babe born under a new star,
And the ancient bondage of the Serpent:
The Word and the Lie.

"All this will I give thee if thou wilt
      but fall down and worship me."
All this:
All these palaces and orchards,
All these rubber plantations and oil fields,
All these factories and tanks and planes.
London, Washington, Paris, Moscow;
Behold, I will give thee this new atomic plant.
In the day that ye eat of this fruit
Ye shall be as God and not die.

Coventry, Dresden, Hamburg, Hiroshima –
Under this betrayal
The earth spins in blood and tears,
Earth and man and man's master,
The machine of civilisation, lashed to the wheel
Of the warfare of two spirits.

"The world situation" we say,
"The world situation is –"
The world situation is the situation of each human heart.

It is not atomic warfare.
There is something less visible than the atom,
Not protons and electrons are the forces,
Spirit and spirit locked in deadly combat
Within the atom, and in the blood, in the mind,
      in the atmosphere.

Not war in the stratosphere,
But war in the atmosphere
Decides.
War in the atmosphere, in the vacuum of man.

He who came once, as babe in a poor stable,
Comes ever anew to hearts that are empty,
Bringing the certainty of final peace.
Light of the new star,
Flame of Love, making the iron red hot,
Hammer on the anvil of brotherhood,
Ploughshares and pruning hooks,
Justice of fellowship,
The murmur of a rushing wind.

Only in a stable, the Word is born,
Not in hearts too full of palaces,
Too full of orchards, and rubber plantations –
There was no room in the inn.

Starlight in a stable, and a new-born babe,
The Word, the I AM.
Heaven and earth shall pass away,
But My Word shall not pass away.

ADVENT 1947

Some work beyond our human power

If millions of war-weary survivors had hoped that the
fall of Germany and Japan in 1945 would herald a new era
of peace, they were to be disappointed. Intense rivalries
between the United States and the Soviet Union devel-
oped into what was soon being called the Cold War, and
fear of atomic warfare gripped the nations. In February
1948 Philip drafted the following article for *Fellowship,*
the magazine of the Fellowship of Reconciliation. It
was never published. Just as he had counselled caution
towards the developments of the Green Revolution,
Philip now warned other pacifists to be wary of the idea
that the great scientific achievements of the last half-cen-
tury would usher in spiritual and intellectual progress. It
would always be a mistake to place hope in the goodness
and abilities of humanity.

In the Time of the Breaking of Nations

Are we standing at the beginning of a new age of
scientific development, of supersonic speeds, of atomic
energy, of more and more wonderful machines? Or are
we standing, unaware, at the end of the machine age, at
the end of the progress of scientific power? Are we about
to enter an era of greater wealth, greater luxury, greater

leisure, the modern home, people emancipated from drudgery? Or has this age of power reached its climax, and will this civilisation destroy itself with those forces which it has created?

Time alone will answer this question, but let us at least be aware that there is a question – that the future is in the balance, and it is by no means certain that the scales will tip for peace and plenty.

To reject this question, to sail onwards in the arrogant confidence that man can and will manipulate these tremendous forces for the good of all, is to put more pressure on the drift to catastrophe. Is not this the poison of the age, the belief of man in man? "Man is certainly stark mad," said Montaigne, "He cannot make a flea, and yet he will be making gods by dozens."

Yet many people have the question in their hearts, and many, many people are haunted by the fear of another war. Some people think another war will mean the end of civilisation, and some people think that civilisation will recover in a nobler, purer form. But the question has even been raised, by L.P. Jacks, "If atomic energy is used for peaceful ends, will the ensuing prosperity destroy mankind no less surely than atomic warfare?" All this leads to a further question: Is man himself making spiritual progress; is he, together with his indisputable intellectual enlightenment, becoming a more noble creature?

Today man can speak and his voice be carried instantaneously to a hundred million listeners, thousands of miles apart – but has he anything to say that is more vital for the welfare of humanity than what Isaiah, or Plato, proclaimed with the unaided voice? . . .

Let it never be denied that sometimes a word of shining wisdom is spoken and printed. There is gold amongst the dross. But if one speaks of humankind making progress, one speaks and dreams of humankind as a whole: in one's mind is a vision of the human race, very gradually, and perhaps even with up-and-down spirals, but very gradually, as a race, rising to nobler heights.

Against this conception of man's spiritual evolution a mountain of evidence is piling up. Some things have been greatly publicised: the concentration camps, lynchings in 1947 in the United States, the rapidly increasing divorce rates, the bombing of Hiroshima, and the continued manufacture of atomic bombs in the post-war armaments race.

But those who put their trust in progress reply that these horrors which mar our civilisation are committed by a relative few. The average man is more enlightened, kindlier, more humane than his remoter forbears. Progress is slow, and sometimes interrupted by the backsliding of a certain nation. On the whole, though, we have made great strides in education, and in the care of the mentally and physically diseased, and in our provisions for social relief. We have definitely become more conscious of our interdependence, and we have done great things in organisation and collaboration.

And there are these veins of gold in the mental output of the world. It would be hard to say if they are more than formerly, or are increasing, but they are more efficiently disseminated. They reach a better educated public, they come from better educated minds. Though it doesn't seem to be invariably so that the sublimest truths are uttered by the best-trained minds, and it would be hard to prove that the gold is purer than it was in the past.

"Be ye all like-minded, compassionate, loving as brethren, tender-hearted, humble-minded" (1 Peter 3:8). This was written by a fisherman in the year 63. Has anything more valuable to humankind been said by any philosopher or theologian in the twentieth century?

Strangely enough, it isn't so much by looking at other people around us that we have become so convinced of this upward trend of humanity. Conviction is carried most strongly home to our heart by looking at ourselves. We know that we have ascended above barbarism. We feel deep within us that, however imperfect we are, we are humane and kindly people. We are seekers for truth, and we live according to our lights. We have our ideals, and we strive to be an influence for good in the world.

But there is a skeleton in our cupboard – the skeleton of an ape. Half of our restless pressing onwards, half of our so frantically clothing ourselves with knowledge, culture, civilisation, is caused by our need to fly from the skeleton of this ancestral ape. We want to put as much distance as possible between us and the past. We want to prove to ourselves that we have left the ape behind. And in the course of our progress we commit atrocities more hideous than any of nature's cruelest beasts could dream of. The character of the beast of prey dominates world society, a beast of prey not only empowered with tremendous physical resources, but empowered with a highly trained intellect to serve his malicious ends.

There is no skeleton in the cupboard. The beast is alive within us. There is no possibility of leaving him behind, of climbing to peaks he cannot reach. We can either fight him or submit to his rule. But within us also, or rather, ready to enter every open heart, is the spirit which fights against the beast, the spirit of the New

Man. And the fight is a choice, with which we are faced every day, and in which we have free will to choose: Which spirit shall I serve?

Our only choice is a choice of service. All our sparkling ability, our insight, our psycho-physical resources, are drawn into the service of one or the other. Our privilege as humans, and our great responsibility, is that we are free to choose. But let us beware of trying to choose both. Let us beware of the fallacy of thinking we can serve the Good on the whole while submitting to the rule of the beast in some small sides of life, or that we can serve the Good with one part of our nature, perhaps the nobler part, while another, more selfish part pays tribute to another god. We have been warned, "You cannot serve two masters, you cannot serve God and mammon" (Matt. 6:24). Let us beware of thinking that life can be divided into departments, the religious and the secular, business and faith. Let us beware of trying to go both ways – for they lead in opposite directions.

What are the manifestations of the beast? Are they confined to the much-publicised and shocking evils of the world? These are only the end products, the ripe fruit of a tree of many branches; the fruit by which we know the tree is evil. The beast is far more cunning. Before it produces fruit the tree has a thousand leaves, a thousand harmless-looking buds, a thousand slender feeder roots which ramify the earth. And it is a great tree. Its height reaches up unto the heaven, and the sight thereof to the ends of the earth, under which the beasts of the earth dwell, and upon whose branches the fowls of the heaven have their habitation (Dan. 4:20–21). Does the beast include then all the personal sins and all the vices? As in the days of Jesus, more than this. The sins that all good people recognise, and some very good people, like the

Pharisees, abjure, are not the most dangerous weapons of the beast. The most dangerous thing about the beast is that he can use our good for his evil.

Our self-respect he turns into class distinction; not necessarily monetary rank – although that often comes in by the back door – but in degrees of virtue by which we disassociate ourselves from others: "I thank Thee that I am not as other men are" (Luke 18:11). It leads on to social class distinctions, it supports them and vindicates them wherever the possession of money, influence, or power is respected – as if the acquisition of it were a measure of a person's worth.

Our appreciation of nobleness and truth he can turn into the worship of man, of a human personality. The basic goodness of man, the "Good Man," the lovely person, are set up before us. Anything to divert us from realising that only the Spirit of God, not the spirit of man, can withstand the beast. Jesus, the perfect man, saw through the significant danger of this when he said, "Why callest thou me good? There is none good but one, that is, God" (Matt. 19:17). Even our zeal for social reform the beast can turn to his own ends, by letting us patch up the rotten system, that it may grind out its injustices without complete collapse – by letting us add a few more fair leaves to the tree which in due time brings forth its evil fruit.

Of course he plays on our weaknesses, our secret faults. But we are aware of this, and are on our guard. But he plays, too, on weaknesses which we either do not realise, or do not wish to admit. We are too proud to admit that we are subject to pride. We are too cowardly to admit, even to ourselves, that we are driven by fear. Pride and fear: he plays on both with the promises of success and security: "I will give you the kingdoms of the world" (Matt. 4:8–10). Democracy must triumph. Let us make the world safe for decent people. It is the desire for security on the part of the average respectable family man that makes war possible. It is the desire to be right and prove it that makes every war a just war – for both sides.

War, and the bestialities that accompany it, wholesale murder and destruction, are the final fruits of the tree that the beast has planted. War is the extreme expression of division between people. War occurs when nothing more unites them, when there is no longer any common ground, any room for negotiation, when people are so utterly divided that there is nothing left but for the one to try and exterminate the other. But people are beguiled into this catastrophic trap by countless tiny steps of division. It begins way back in the virtuous little disassociations of oneself from the weaknesses that are all too evident in one's neighbour. Every tiny stage of division, of separation, is a step towards war. Division in all its forms is the weapon of the beast. All the subtle barriers of mine and thine, pride and fear, certainly, and all their relatives: ambition, self-esteem, indifference to others, my responsibility as steward of my goods, and so on.

In absolute opposition to what we have been calling the spirit of the beast is the Spirit of Love. This spirit alone can bring that peace which is in absolute opposition to war and death and destruction. Peace which is born of love and filled with love is the only true peace. It is not just a cessation of war, a shaking of the ripe fruit while the tree goes on growing to bear again in due season. Peace can only arise when the tree is cut down and rooted out. In this mighty work, love uses weapons which are in absolute opposition to the weapons of the beast. Instead of the Good Man, the

poor in spirit; instead of the confidence in the progress
of man, the sorrowful recognition of the helplessness of
man; instead of the mighty, the meek; instead of self-sat-
isfaction, the hungering and thirsting for righteousness;
instead of judgement, mercy; instead of the doctrine of
many paths, singleness and pureness of heart; instead of
coercion, reconciliation; instead of success, persecution
for righteousness' sake.

Against the multiple weapons of division, love builds
the fortress of unity. This, too, has its foundations way
down in the practical things of daily life. Mine and thine
are done away with, in material as in spiritual things.
Property divides people, the haves from the have-nots-
or not-so-much. It is one of the first barriers that melts
in the glow of love. But individual pride and self-respect
are properties of the heart. They vanish too, in the
realisation that we are all weak, and there is none good
but God; that we are all brothers and sisters and one
is our master, even Christ. We are no longer separated
individuals, each with a slightly different "kingdom of
God" within us. But we are all members of one body,
with a common purpose, and a common source of
strength to follow it. Thus each shares with the other,
goods and work and table, for everything belongs to the
Spirit of Love. Each helps the other, and accepts help, for
the victory is not unto us. There arises brotherhood, as
our true calling, as the fruit of the Spirit of Love, as the
unity which establishes peace.

The victory is not unto us, but the fight cuts us to
the marrow. Peace is not the achievement of man, but
of the Spirit of Love, of God. But the Spirit demands
our unconditional surrender to his government, and we
do not like unconditional surrender. The beast seems
to demand far less: "If thou wilt but bow down and

worship me" (Matt.4:9). He will allow us to go on being good people, doing good works. You only have to give him the little finger. You may meditate on the most exalted ideals of the brotherhood of all men, you may speak and write about them, you may preach them to others – as long as you don't actually live out full brotherhood with any man. Even in this you may go a long way, you may be cooperative, you may have a "spiritual brotherhood," as long as you leave that little finger. But to go the whole way, you yourself, with your own flesh and blood, that's a different kettle of fish. Unconditional surrender, denying the beast down to the soles of your boots, that's what cuts to the marrow. Yet that is the choice that Jesus puts before us throughout his teaching, wriggle how we may. "Take up thy cross and follow me" (Mark 8:34), "leave father and mother" (Mark 10:29), "let the dead bury their dead" (Matt. 8:22), "sell all that thou hast" (Luke 18:22) – no compromise! It is far easier to say "Lord, Lord."

It is far easier to say "Lord, Lord," and much more respected. Yet there is always this insistence of Jesus upon deeds, not words. Even the cup of water to the least of these my brethren (Matt. 10:42). One drop of life-blood spent in the actual practice of brotherhood is more effective in the struggle for peace than an ocean of ink writing about it. This would not be true perhaps if victory lay within the power of man, if the struggle were one of human goodwill against human weakness, of human progress against our obscure origins; if the kingdom of God could be set up by man. The faith that an ounce of action is worth a ton of speech, the faith that there can be any significance whatever in a tiny group of very ordinary people trying to live brotherhood, can rest only on the faith in the living God. That God acts, and that his will is love, his purpose peace on the earth, is the justification for the decision to put that will wholly into practice in our lives here and now. It is the significance of the savour of the salt. The vital thing is not the bulk of the substance, but that the salt be salt.

Community is not a system for solving the economic-social problem. Many such communities have been organised and have failed to stay the course. Community is a consequence. Community is the consequence of people being kindled with the glow of love. Community is the consequence when people see right through to the depths the necessity of the fundamental choice, either/or. Either unity or division, either brotherhood or war. It is when people see this choice and, having seen it, make the choice to serve the Spirit of Love in terms of unconditional surrender, that they are drawn together, that they are given community through the power of love. A new form of society emerges because people are filled with a new spirit. Community cannot exist in the absence of the Spirit of Love. Love cannot be expressed where there is division, competition, isolation, egotism. Each one must give himself wholeheartedly to all – making no reservations. "The kingdom of God is within you" (Luke 17:21). This sentence has been twisted by the religion of this world to blind us to the real and concrete issues. The kingdom of God is not a comfortable feeling inside that we have attained a harmony of our souls with abstract truth. Above all, the kingdom of God is not the private property of each individual soul. The kingdom of God is the reign of God on this earth. To the words, "Thy kingdom come," belong the words, "Thy will be done on earth . . ." (Matt. 6:10).

Instead of the glittering palace of manifold divisions, let us seek a simple house with an open door. Instead of the towering organisation of worldly skill and worldly knowledge, let us seek a humble trust in God. Let us make the unconditional surrender to the Spirit of Love. "Except a man be born again he cannot enter the kingdom of heaven" (John 3:3). Let us beware of trying to save ourselves by going the two ways. "He who seeks his life shall lose it" (Matt. 10:39). Are we standing at the brink of long vistas of prosperous evolution, or is civilisation moving towards its own destruction? Has it the seeds of life or death within it? Our only choice is a choice of service, and service means deed, not word. It is either/or. Serve one or the other. Prune the great tree of division or plant the new tree of brotherhood. Let us not be misled by the symptoms of human power. The power of God alone is decisive in the end.

Even as the possibility of a new war grew, many in Europe were still in desperate circumstances following the last war. What could they do to help? The community had never given up hope that somehow the children's village they had built could be used for its intended purpose. Then, in February 1948, they received a request from the International Refugee Organization in Geneva to take in more than a hundred displaced persons.

The community gathered for a meeting. Philip quoted from Psalm 9: "The Lord is become a refuge for the poor: a helper in due time of tribulation. . . . He hath not forgotten the cry of the poor." He continued:

> The group of 114 is numerically insignificant compared with the 800,000 who need homes. . . .

Although the building of houses, the extension of agriculture, the collection or making of equipment has strained our resources, has caused us much hard work and many headaches, these things are not the most important. . . . What will be decisive when the group arrives . . . will be the spirit in which we live, as expressed in our deeds and in our whole attitude.

The light of the love of God must shine clearly through us, and there must be no shadow of discontent.

The community decided to take refugees who would be willing to remain and work for one year. Not wanting to hide the difficulties of life in Paraguay, they sent a letter describing their living circumstances, and then, once again, found themselves waiting for an answer.

The summer of 1947 1948 had been very hot and dry. The locusts had finally grown their wings and flown away, but the drought continued through January, withering the remnants of crops in the devastated fields and gardens. It was one of Paraguay's worst droughts in a hundred years.

Around this time, Philip's symptoms recurred: he was again having trouble with indigestion, and ulcers in his mouth. Following the same treatment he had received the previous year, his indigestion improved, though the sores remained. At least there was relief from the drought: February brought thunderstorms and heavy rain, and the community's farmers could replant the crops.

THE CORN CROP

When clouds swept low the sky at morn,
We planted seed of golden corn,
Stoop low, stoop low.
Upon the newly planted earth
Fell rain to bring the seed to birth,
That maketh corn to grow.

We watched the corn grow tall and green,
We hoed the stubborn weed between,
Stoop low, stoop low.
Some work beyond our human power,
By sun and rain brought forth the flower,
That maketh corn to grow.

The grain grew fat upon the stalk,
The farmers talked the harvest talk,
Stoop low, stoop low.
Now praise to God who by his might
Hath made the harvest golden bright,
Who maketh corn to grow.

1948

SONNET II

Let us not forget the durability of hardwood,
Not having the elegance of chromium plate,
But mellowing slowly. Lasting not so long
As comes one flash of light from star Antares –
Yet in a man's life they will scarcely change.
Let us not forget, the apple tree is an old tree,
Yet every spring the orchard blooms anew,
Not like neon lights, but changing slowly,
Changing with a stir of things beyond,
Responsive to a rhythm that swings the Scorpion,
Swings, too, our hearts, like the pull of tides.
Let us build rather by what eternal pulse
Swings high the sap; by what gigantic hand
Holds blood and sap and planet in its palm.

1948

Quicken the seed
In the dark, damp earth.
Nourish our need,
God of all birth.
Thou art the seed
That we bury now.
Thou art our need,
God of the plough.
Bury the spark
Of our own desire
Deep in the dark,
God of the fire.
After the night
When the fight is won,
Thou art the light,
God of the sun.

EASTER 1948

Here is a mystery

At Easter, as the community gathered for a festive
meal, Philip spoke passionately of what it means to be a
follower of Jesus:

> We do not discover Jesus and elect him as our leader,
> but he discovers us and calls us. He calls us to this way
> and removes the scales from our eyes that we might
> see it. All that we can do is to obey and follow. To obey
> Jesus means to forsake our old lives and live henceforth
> only his life; to leave our boats and our nets by the sea
> and follow him in new ways; to wander with him, be
> it through desert or city; to hang upon his words, and
> to give witness to our faith that he is the Light of the
> World, and he alone.
>
> To follow Jesus is complete surrender of our posses-
> sions, our claims on life, our own wills and our very
> safety, for the sake of his message to humankind.
>
> To follow Jesus is to live this message with our own
> life-blood and to call other people that they also live it as
> the one hope of peace.
>
> When we follow the call of Jesus, when we really
> leave our boats behind us, as did the first disciples, the
> Spirit of Jesus, the Holy Spirit, walks with us. Were
> it not so, we could never find the way. This Spirit is
> overflowing love to all people. . . .

For the despairing and the oppressed we are given a message of hope: there is a way that leads to renewed life. Love was slain, but love is stronger than death. The risen Christ brings the nearness of God and his renewing life to people as never before. Jesus opens out the new way of God into the world, for now the contrast between his love and the unity of his life, and our world, has been revealed.

For the proud and prosperous, for the worldly wise and worldly powerful, we are given a message of warning: the worldly life bears within it the seeds of its own judgement and will bring forth the fruit of its own destruction. . . .

We are called to proclaim to all people, to the rich and the poor, the message of the kingdom of God. That it shall be established not by our upward climbing, but by the coming down of Christ; not by organisation and reform, but by the power of love that surrenders and sacrifices itself unto death.

Two weeks later, by the middle of April 1948, Philip's mouth was so inflamed that he could hardly speak. He lost weight and began running a fever, and spent a week in the community's hospital. Back at home, he was still weak, unable to eat solid food. "I wish they could do something for him," Joan said sadly to her neighbour once. "I hear him moan at night." What was hardest for him was seeing tasks that needed doing and not being able to help. But he continued to write.

Activity and Contemplation

"It is good to be busy," writes Silesius,* "and better to pray, but far better yet to stand mute and still before your God."

This the poets have always sung, and this is the task and meaning of poetry: to represent values other than those which can be measured in work done or profit gained.

But there must be work too. Both activity and contemplation are part of true living. Augustine says, "One may not be so given to contemplation that he forgets the good of his neighbour, nor so much in love with action that he forgets divine speculation."

The good of his neighbour: that is the call to action. I believe this action will be more full of joyous, spontaneous love if we have come near to the glory of him who is love, in contemplation; if we have felt something of his love warming our souls as sunshine warms the body. And without that love, action is nothing.

"Though I speak with the tongues of men and of angels, and have not love – I am nothing. Though I have faith to remove mountains, though I give my body to be burned, and have not love – I am nothing" (1 Cor. 13:1–3).

There are mountains to be removed, and the greatest are within our own hearts: the mountains of self-love and pride and fear. Let us not make a mole hill out of these mountains, for they are truly gigantic. They are the foundations of all the coldness and injustice and hate and violence in the world. And we can make no headway against these world-spread evils unless we first remove – cast out and into the sea – those mountains of pride and self-love within ourselves. But if we do set

---

* Angelus Silesius (1624–1677), born Johannes Scheffler, was a German Catholic priest, physician, mystic, and poet.

about removing these personal mountains, we cannot
leave it at that but must immediately project the same
determination outwards. . . .

In June, in another attempt to find a cure – or at least a
diagnosis – Philip travelled to the Hospital for Infectious
Diseases in Asunción. This time, the doctor diagnosed
paracoccidiosis brasiliensis, a rare and deadly disease
caused by a fungus in the soil of southeast Brazil, where
Philip had been in 1945.

The Primavera doctors sought advice from tropical
disease institutes abroad, hoping to find effective
treatment. Philip and Joan and their children were
given rooms in a brick house known for its coolness.
When the heat of the summer increased, Philip found
it hard to leave his room. One day he admitted to Chris
Caine how much the heat bothered him, but added with
determination, "Self-pity, self-pity – never, never let it
come anywhere near you to make the littlest beginning
with you. If you let it come just a little bit close to you, it
takes you with it and runs away with you like a roaring
waterfall." His arms came crashing down to demonstrate.

With his illness increasingly confining him to the
house, Philip had more time to write. "Behind Nature"
encapsulates one of the themes that runs through his
writing and agricultural work: "The deeper we have
pursued knowledge of these things, the greater must be
our wonder and humility before the mystery of life."

Behind Nature

Here in this wild land, we have many opportunities to sense the power of God in nature.

When the great thunderstorms roll up, and the lightning splits the sky above us, with thunder like the crack of doom, when flash follows flash, and explosion follows explosion, each one mightier than the last, and the wind rises with increasing violence – in our hearts is the whisper, "How much fiercer will it get? How much stronger can it get? Is there a limit to this awful display of power?" And we do not know if there is a limit, but we know we are utterly helpless to stop or change it.

But God is over all.

Here we can feel our smallness and helplessness before God. Here all our illusions of strength and sufficiency wither, wilt, and vanish in the realisation of our nothingness.

"What is man that thou shouldst heed him?" (Ps. 8:4).

But let us stand also in a field of maize in flower, watching the sheen of sunlight on the leaves and the nodding tassels, remembering how, four days after we had planted the grain, the soft green feathers pushed through the soil.

Here is life, here is something far beyond our greatest achievements. Here is a mystery we do not understand. The more we know about it, the greater is the mystery. As we stand there we realise how the roots are drawing water and nutriments from the soil; how countless micro-organisms are preparing those nutriments from the tissues of other dead plants; how the leaves are taking carbon from the air and manufacturing starch and sugar and cellulose and vitamins; how tiny things, so small that no one has seen them yet passed on from

parent to progeny, are controlling the ability of the
plant to do this. The more we realise all this, the more
keenly we are aware of this mystery, the deeper we have
pursued knowledge of these things, the greater must be
our wonder and humility before the mystery of life.

Here all our pride of achievement and understanding
dwindles to nothingness in the perception of a vital
force, a wisdom that surrounds us, with the unspoken
words I AM.

"I cannot believe in miracles," said a young man
once to a young woman who was preparing vegetables
for cooking. She cut a cabbage in half and showed it to
him, with all the pattern of the folded leaves, and asked,
"Have you ever tried to make a cabbage?"

A young child believes in miracles, as a natural
or normal part of life, because it sees the miracle in
everything. And in that seeing, that seeing of miracles,
to which our older eyes have become dim, the child is
very near to God. Verily, unless we become as a little
child, we cannot see the kingdom of God (Matt. 18:3).
Let us beware then of doing anything that can pull any
child away from its vision, away from God. If ever we
find that we have no time for the children, that we are
too busy to talk to them, or too tired, let us consider
well what is that business we are about – is it really more
vital than to share time with a child, is it really more our
Father's business?

It takes much less than a thunderstorm or a field of
growing corn to make a child stand in wonder before
God. Who has not seen a child transfixed with wonder
at a butterfly, a beetle, or a mouse-nest in the grass? And
a corn plant, or a stalk of kafir, or a tall flowering reed
is a thing to be carried aloft and waved in the sky: it is a
banner, a torch, a lantern.

Plough Quarterly

FREE TRIAL ISSUE

Thank you for your purchase. If you liked this book, you'll want to try our magazine as well. Plough Quarterly brings together a diverse community of readers serious about putting their faith into action. And since you bought one of our books, we'd like to offer one issue free.

Give it a try! Just drop this completed card in the mail, and we'll send you a free trial issue. No cost, no obligation. If you like it, you'll get four more issues for just $18. If you decide not to subscribe, simply write "cancel" on the invoice, return it, and owe nothing. Either way, the trial issue is yours to keep.

Name

Address

City   State   Zip

Email (We will not share your email address with any third party)

BUSINESS REPLY MAIL

FIRST–CLASS MAIL PERMIT NO. 332 CONGERS, NY

POSTAGE WILL BE PAID BY ADDRESSEE

PLOUGH QUARTERLY
PO BOX 345
CONGERS NY 10920–9895

If we can capture some of this childlike astonishment, we shall learn more of the kingdom of God. Let us not make the mistake of capitalist civilisation by considering our human business the sum of life. This error is responsible for who knows how much need, how much starvation of soul, how much lack of light.

Like water at the roots

Primavera was receiving more and more letters from the United States enquiring about the community: Does it work? If it does, how does it work? What is the secret? Unable to do physical work, Philip turned his energies to responding to these letters and to taking time with visitors. On August 29, 1948, he spoke at a gathering of guests:

> This is the meaning of brotherhood – not a haven of refuge, but a joyous aggression against all wrong.
>
> This is also the difference between the new life in the Spirit of Jesus and all other forms of life.
>
> This life is not based on laws or dogma, nor any code, nor creed of righteous living. Life is lifted above any set of rules, even good rules of living. Life is lived by the ever-renewed experience of the Spirit – infinite in the variety of its ways, yet never contradicting itself. The law and the prophets are not done away with, but they are fulfilled.
>
> The work of this Spirit is glowing love: first towards God – who is life, who is love itself – and then from this towards all people. It means the complete surrender of self to outgoing and outpouring love, not a soft and sentimental love in the smoky fires of our own feeling. Love

is going out from ourselves. Love is living for God – the dedication of our whole being to the service of life.

In this love we must call all people to an utterly different way of life. Away from the dog-eat-dog of competitive living. Pit your strength no longer against each other but unreservedly for each other, and especially for the poor and weak. Away from the hypocrisy of a religion that does not penetrate all relationships. Let us live out all that we recognise as good, even when it sears our flesh. Away from the limitation and the coldness of property and selfish living! To the cry, "Lay down your weapons," belongs the cry, "Take up your tools." Put your words into practice; put your good intentions into the reality of living.

You will find it hard going sometimes, but we will go it together. Brotherhood is not a panacea for the problems of life. The struggle is intensified, not lessened. But mutual aid in the driving power of love brings the strength and joy of unity. Let each add one more torch to the fire, that the light of brotherhood – of actual, living, all-out brotherhood – may shine clearly and warmly in the chilly darkness of our times.

For the first time in years, Philip now had uninterrupted stretches of time to write essays like this one:

Plants in the Tropical Sunlight

We go forward in faith, on tasks which we know
are humanly impossible, in the face of opposition so
powerful that our human courage droops like a plant
in dry soil. Our activity, our human works, are like the
life of a plant. You have all seen a field of maize wilting
and drooping in a blazing sun. Each plant is active, each

plant is growing and maturing to produce fruit. If there
is not enough water in the soil, the plant withers in the
heat of the midday sun, because it is giving out water
faster than it can find it with its roots. The sun is sucking
water from the leaves, and the roots cannot replace
it. But if water is given to the roots, the plant revives
and grows, and turns that very sunlight into cells and
chlorophyll, and finally into flowers and fruit.

We are like plants in the tropical sunlight. The
fierceness of the sun is like the judgement of God,
revealing everything, burning, purifying. Here faith is
like water at the roots. If we have faith, we can face the
sun, we can turn the heat and the light into life-giving
fruits, into love.

Here we must remember a vital difference between
faith and taking things for granted. Faith is always a
gift, while the other is human confidence which leaves
the working of God within the scope and grasp of
human imagination – which forgets that his ways are
higher than our ways and his thoughts higher than our
thoughts. Faith is a gift like the rain, and like the rain
it is something to be watched for and prayed for and
waited for.

We cannot produce it, and we cannot make it come.
But in fellowship of community we can help each other
to find it. He who has received faith can encourage
the others, as one can give a plant water with a water-
ing-can. But ultimately we are dependent on the grace of
God for faith just as plants are dependent on the grace of
God for rain.

No plant can live without the rhythm of day and
night, and we too, as human beings, need the rhythm
of rest and action. Just as the plant uses the hours of the
night to recover from the giving out of strength in the

day, and to refresh itself with dew, so we also need these times of withdrawal and of quiet.

But the plant does not cease to live or to grow in the night, and for us, too, the times of relative quiet and withdrawal should be times of activity, though of a different kind. We need to seek times when we quieten our hearts and minds, in order to receive and absorb the refreshing word of God, the voice of God calling to our hearts, the Spirit of God moving in our minds.

At such times our activity is one of listening and of prayer, from which we draw both clarity and courage for further action. Then we go out strengthened and resolved to carry on the battle, to walk in God's ways, to bear witness to the cry of the prophets, in the strength of the Son of Man.

This is the meaning of our meetings together, that the heart meets God and experiences the power of him who is for us, who is greater than he who is against us. We need to do this more often than we can meet together, especially when we are parted from each other, on long and hard journeys, when we are placed almost alone among the powers of the world, when we are surrounded by that power which does not repent of the works of its hands, nor cease from the worship of idols of gold, silver, and stone. On such tasks we need to turn often to the refreshing dew of meeting with God. . . .

Just as many plants perform their most important work at night, in the hours of quietness, like the sorghum, or kafir, which flowers during the hour or two before sunrise, so in our time of turning to God in prayer our most important task is done. In these hours the decisive thing happens, which governs all that we may do in the heat of the day.

All our running around and speaking with important people cannot bear the true result, unless God works with us and for us. "Unless the Lord build the house, they labour in vain that build it" (Ps. 127:1).

These two things alone can maintain us in that love which overcomes the world: the meeting with God in our hearts – in the heart of each one of us and the united heart of all – and faith which is given as the rain from heaven. We must watch and wait and pray for faith: we must open our hearts for faith as water that feeds the roots.

Thankfully, the locusts did not return that summer. Milk
production increased, the crops were flourishing, and
that was a joy to Philip. He and Joan were expecting their
fourth child. In the cool of their house they listened to
classical music from a hand-cranked gramophone and
spent every moment they could with their children. The
next poem vividly captures one such moment.

TOUCAN

The boy there,
Standing, staring,
Staring at the bird –
Eyes alight, breath held,
Bare toes gripping the sand,
Wonder-held.
The boy there,
Standing, staring –
That's my son –
A sound from me
And he will turn,
Dart to me,
"Daddy, did you see?"

1948

"This was probably the last poem Philip wrote," Joan noted when she copied it out for a friend, "at the end of October or early November, 1948, when he and Simon saw a toucan together."

The community continued preparations for the displaced persons, who arrived in early November. Philip took part in communal activities as much as possible, though he was weak. During the Christmas celebrations, he organised a cricket match, and was the captain of one team. He played with great enthusiasm, but had to sit out a short while to rest.

In the meantime, the continuing wave of visitors from North America, and the growing interest in community living that they represented, had prompted serious discussions about Primavera's obligations beyond Paraguay. Could a trip to the United States, Philip wondered, combine two purposes: to raise funds for Primavera's charitable hospital and to meet people searching for answers after the war? The decision had been put off, but finally, on January 9, 1949, two men were chosen to make a trip to North America. Philip helped make a list of names and addresses of people who might be eager to host the two. On January 16, he spoke in a meeting:

> Our first and great responsibility is to "love the Lord our God with all our heart, with all our mind, and with all our strength, and the second is like it–to love our neighbours as if they were ourselves" (Mark 12:30–31). . . . Let our lives and every word spoken and every consideration of all matters, personal and communal, of work and of emotion, and every deed be governed by this faith in our almighty Father, who is all goodness, all truth, and all love. . . . Let us thank God for these responsibilities,

let us shoulder them gladly, and let us ask him for the strength to carry them faithfully.

On Sunday, January 22, 1949, Philip spoke in a meeting about his wish to compile a book so that the witness of the community might better reach North America. A second visitor from the United States had asked to join the community, and the letters of interest had kept coming. "Philip was so alive and so full of ideas," one of his friends remembered later, "that one had not the faintest idea that he must have been already so ill. He was so unconscious of himself. His whole mind and all his thoughts were in the task."

But during the following week, Philip developed a high fever and stomach pain. On Sunday, the doctor diagnosed peritonitis: part of Philip's abdominal tissue was infected. They decided to operate, to see if the infected tissue could be removed. When they began the operation, they soon realised that they could not save Philip's life: the infection and the lesions from the disease had spread too far.

One of the doctors, a recent refugee from Eastern Europe whom Philip had befriended, was so shaken that he did not leave his house for the next three days.

At 1:30 in the morning of January 31, 1949, the community was called together to pray for Philip. He died later the same day. He was thirty-one years old.

"Philip bore this illness for years with no complaining," Arthur Woolston, the community's pharmacist, later wrote. "To the last, in great pain, he suffered silently, giving no indication of what agonies he must have had. We all had a great love and respect for Philip. . . . He showed us such an example of work, humility, and understanding."

The next day, at a meal after his funeral, Hans Meier spoke for many when he recalled Philip's life:

> Philip did not like to stand in the forefront; it was his custom to be in the background until he was called on. He represented among us a more inward, almost mystical aspect of life, but he did this in a healthy way. . . .
>
> He was a man matured through inward and outward suffering and also through suffering with others. He had a special interest in nature, as a book of God in which one could read of the wisdom of God and the nature of God. He never devoted himself in a mechanical way to agriculture, but loved it for the sake of the mystery of life which he sensed and experienced there. In his teaching of biology to the children here he tried to impart something of this. . . .
>
> Philip had a very keen sense of what is essential. He felt that one should not only discern between good and evil, but that where something is blurred and unclear, one should seek out the good that is there.

Joan spoke a few words to the community as well:

> This morning . . . I was reading Philip's letters – and through those long absences I have many letters – and what was important for us was that we see the small things as small, and the great things as great, and I think that one must not go down under a flood of sorrow. Ever since we have known each other, we always felt that we had been led together by God. Always there came a certain point when we knew we must do something and we did it, and now I begin to feel that it was right of God to take him in the middle of his great activity, because I feel that was the true thing, that this person who was so full of life and love is how we must remember him.

Still, it was a crushing blow for Joan, then five months pregnant. In the months after his death, she sorted through his papers. As she faced the uncertainties and pain of childbirth alone, discovering a new poem or finding an old favourite in Philip's own hand was a comfort.

The community was left reeling as well. Few had realised the gravity of his illness, and suddenly he was gone. As well as leaving his wife a widow, and his children fatherless, he left a community without a pastor, his practical and intellectual work barely begun.

When little Philip was born May 13, 1949, the whole community rejoiced.

In 1953 Joan married Leonard Pavitt, a community member and friend of Philip's. They had a daughter, Joan, born the following year.

Meanwhile, the ties to the United States that Philip had advocated grew stronger; the seeds he had sown bore fruit. By 1954 there was a Bruderhof community in New York, and in 1955 Joan and Leonard moved there with their five children.

After deciding to leave the community in 1959, the couple eventually returned to England, where Joan died in 1981. Philip and Joan's children now live in the United States, England, and Australia.

It is thanks to Joan that so many of Philip's essays and poems are preserved. She collated and copied out his poetry, by hand, over and over, as gifts to their friends. For, as she noted on the flyleaf of one such collection, "Herein the heart and mind of my/our Philip lie revealed."

Philip and
Joan Britts at
the Cotswold
Bruderhof

EPILOGUE

Forty years after Philip's death, this poem was
discovered, carefully written out, among the papers of
fellow community member Hardy Arnold. It is undated,
but was accompanied by this note:

> Dear Hardy,
>
> I think that at last I have written something which is
> not only out of my personal experience, but out of the
> common experience, and therefore I have great joy in
> giving it to you, and have no fear as to whether it is good
> or bad poetry, but only hope that you, too, will think
> that it expresses something that is moving in the church.
>
> In unity and love,
>
> Philip

THE ETERNAL PEOPLE

I sing of the eternal people,
And the eternal city,
The city of the eternal warfare
Which is the embassy of the ultimate peace.

When a nation sallies against another nation,
With spears or muskets, cannon or tanks,
For a year or for a generation,
That is not the true warfare,
Nor is that the eternal city.

And when one has proved itself the stronger,
And politicians ponder terms of peace,
And armies are recalled, and penalties are paid,
And the normal national life begins again
In pride or in humiliation,
That is not the true peace, the ultimate peace.

The combat ends and slowly is forgotten,
The political peace is sooner or later broken,
And sooner or later the city and the people become only
   a memory.

But the eternal people,
In the eternal city,
They wage the eternal warfare
Because they are the embassy of the ultimate peace.

Is the eternal city full of gilded towers?
Are the streets broad and paved with marble?
Is she defended by gates of steel that endure?
And are her palaces of polished gold?

And the eternal people, are they strong?
Are they comely, are they stately in their walk?
Are they keener of intellect than other men,
And have they greater courage?

No, but the eternal city is other than this,
And the eternal people are other than this.

At times the city is a group of plaster cottages,
At times the city is built of wood with roofs of grass,
At times the city is a circle of tents pitched by a river.
At times the city is a clearing in a forest, with watch-fires
    but no houses.

And the eternal people are as other people,
No taller, no braver, no stronger, no cleverer.
In the eternal people many are weak,
Many are slow-thinking, many are timid.
The eternal people are as other people,
Only their eyes are more like the eyes of children,
Shining with the freedom of the eternal city.

Then how is it that this people is eternal?
And how is it that this city is eternal?
Why do they not pass into oblivion,
As all cities and all people pass at last into oblivion?

They are the eternal people
And it is the eternal city
Because they wage the eternal warfare,
Because they are the embassy of the ultimate peace.
They are not strong in themselves, the eternal people,
If they were strong they would be proud
And all that which is proud will perish.
Yet mighty things are done through them,

The hearts of haughty governments are moved,
Deadly seas are sailed across in safety,
And what is mightier than all this –
In the midst of ruinous war they are at peace.

The life of the eternal people
Lies in the hand of the invisible King,
The King who has neither castle nor court,
Who compels no man to be his subject,
Who compels no man to obey his word.
Even this King, the invisible King,
He is the King of the eternal people.

The true warfare, the eternal warfare,
Is not the striving of men against each other,
It is the war of the creator against the destroyer,
It is the war of the will to life against the will to death,
The war of love against hate,
The war of unity against separation
It is the war of the invisible King against the darkness.
Those who wage this war, they are the eternal people
And their city is the eternal city.

And the ultimate peace is the overthrow of all
    destructive forces,
It is the establishment of a new order upon the earth,
An order where love reigns over every aspect of life,
Over the relationships of all men to one another,
Over the actions of all men, towards themselves and
    towards all things outside themselves.
And this peace is established in the hearts of the eternal
    people,
Because they are the embassy of the ultimate peace,
For which they wage the eternal warfare.

The war of the eternal people is a hard war,
And to be one of them is a hard undertaking,
For the enemy attacks each one in his own heart,
And must be fought continually, each in his own blood.
And the hardness of the fight is that the enemy attacks
    in disguise,
He comes as a friend or a champion,
And is beautiful or desirable,
But he is a traitor, and his beauty turns to hideousness.
And the problem of the eternal people is to recognise
    the enemy,
For when he is revealed his power is broken.
This is the victory of the invisible King,
That he unmasks the enemy, and overcomes him.
When the enemy seeks to divide them,
When the enemy tries to deceive them,
He is stronger than the enemy,
And with his burning love he drives him out.

The weapons of the eternal people are not carnal
    weapons,
The weapons of the eternal people are the will to Truth,
The will to unity and the means to unity which is Love
And above all, loyalty to the invisible King.
The strength of the eternal people is that they are not
    divided against each other.
Only that which is undivided is eternal.

Part of the eternal city may be in one country,
And part may be a thousand miles away.
It is not a matter of space,
It is a matter of the unity of heart and mind against the
    common enemy.
And the enemy of the eternal people is the Prince of
    Death.

These are the commands of the invisible King:
That they are not divided against each other,
Either in spiritual pride or in material competition,
But that each sees in the other his comrade in arms,
And has perfect love towards him and helps him in the
fight,
And that they be all brothers fighting side by side the
eternal warfare.
And the measure of the strength of the eternal people
Is the measure of their obedience to the invisible King.

Those who stand beneath the banner of the invisible
King,
They are the eternal people.
They are the people of the eternal warfare,
and they are the embassy of the ultimate peace.

Index of Poem Titles and First Lines

Titles in italics

Related Titles from Plough

Called to Community: The Life Jesus Wants for His People
Charles E. Moore, Ed.

God's Revolution: Justice, Community, and the Coming Kingdom
Eberhard Arnold

Homage to a Broken Man: The Life of J. Heinrich Arnold
Peter Mommsen

A Joyful Pilgrimage: My Life in Community
Emmy Arnold

No Lasting Home: A Year in the Paraguayan Wilderness
Emmy Barth

Salt and Light: Living the Sermon on the Mount
Eberhard Arnold

Want to give this book to a friend? And keep it too?
Now you can: if you pass this book on, we're happy to replace it
for free. For details visit **plough.com/give**.

PLOUGH PUBLISHING HOUSE
PO BOX 398, Walden, NY 12586, USA
Robertsbridge, East Sussex TN32 5DR, UK
4188 Gwydir Highway, Elsmore, NSW 2360, Australia
845-572-3455 • info@plough.com • www.plough.com